THE 3RD SS PANZER REGIMENT

CASEMATE | ILLUSTRATED

CASEMATE | ILLUSTRATED

THE 3RD SS PANZER REGIMENT

3RD SS PANZER DIVISION TOTENKOPF

PIERRE TIQUET

CASEMATE | ILLUSTRATED

I would like to thank my wife for her unflappable patience, as well as Gregory Gochgarian, Roberto Christiani, and Andrii Zubkobv for their help and encouragement.

CIS0011

This book is published in cooperation with and under license from Editions Heimdal. Adapted from *Souvenirs de Vétérans du SS-Pz.-Rgt. 3 "Totenkopf"* © Editions Heimdal, 2017

Print Edition: ISBN 978-1-61200-7311
Digital Edition: ISBN 978-1-61200-7328

Design by Battlefield Design
Color profiles by Battlefield Design
Translated by Hannah McAdams
Printed and bound in the Czech Republic by FINIDR, s.r.o.

CASEMATE PUBLISHERS (US)
Telephone (610) 853-9131
Fax (610) 853-9146
Email: casemate@casematepublishers.com
www.casematepublishers.com

CASEMATE PUBLISHERS (UK)
Telephone (01865) 241249
Fax (01865) 794449
Email: casemate-uk@casematepublishers.co.uk
www.casematepublishers.co.uk

Title page: Panzer III 502, 3rd SS Panzer Regiment Totenkopf. Note that three crewmembers wear the camouflaged overalls of the Waffen-SS. This photo was taken in July 1943 in the Belgorod region. Gunner Werner Söldner has his back turned to the camera.
Contents page: Ernst Walter Kirsch's Panzer Badge (*Panzerkampfabzeichen*) with case, and SS ring.

Note: vehicle illustrations and profiles are not to scale.

Contents

Timeline of Events

The history of the Totenkopf Division is one of two parts—the three-year period from October 1939 to October 1942 when the division was not designated a panzer division, and the period November 1942 to May 1945, when it was. It was in this latter period that the 3rd SS Panzer Regiment was formed.

1942

November 1942: 3rd SS Panzer Regiment formed, in France.

1943

February 1943: Totenkopf Division transferred to the Eastern Front.

February 19, 1943: Third battle of Kharkov opens. 3rd SS Panzer Regiment receives its first Tiger tanks.

March 15, 1943: The third battle of Kharkov closes with a German victory.

July 5, 1943: Operation *Citadel*, the German attempt to close the Kursk salient, opens.

July 14, 1943: With the Wehrmacht having exhausted itself, Hitler shuts down *Citadel*.

August 2, 1943: The Soviets penetrate the Mius Front. After bitter fighting, 3rd SS Panzer Regiment reduced to 20 tanks.

August 3, 1943: 3rd SS Panzer Regiment involved in the fourth battle of Kharkov.

August 23, 1943: Red Army victorious at Kharkov. Totenkopf begins fighting withdrawal to the Dnieper.

November 1943: Totenkopf involved in the battle for Krivoi Rog, lasting several weeks.

Left and opposite: A collection of veterans' decorations on a battered album decorated with an officer's armband. The set includes an Iron Cross 2nd class with original pouch, an Iron Cross 1st class in a presentation box and yellow cardboard outer box, and a bronze Panzer Badge.

1944

February 1944: 3rd SS Panzer Regiment attempts to relieve the Korsun Pocket.

April 4, 1944: 3rd SS Panzer Regiment retreats over the Dniester, into Romania.

May 7, 1944: 3rd SS Panzer Regiment successfully holds the Red Army at the second battle of Târgu Frumos.

July 9, 1944: 3rd SS Panzer Regiment transferred to Poland, fighting for 5 months to halt Soviet Operation *Bagration.*

December 25, 1944: 3rd SS Panzer Regiment transferred to Hungary.

1945

January 1–20, 1945: Operations *Konrad I, II* and *III* launched, to relieve Budapest, but fail.

February 13, 1945: Budapest falls to the Red Army.

May 8, 1945: German unconditional surrender.

May 9, 1945: Totenkopf Division surrenders to 11th U.S. Armored Division, in Czechoslovakia.

May 14, 1945: U.S. forces hand German POWs over to Red Army, to begin transfer to Odessa.

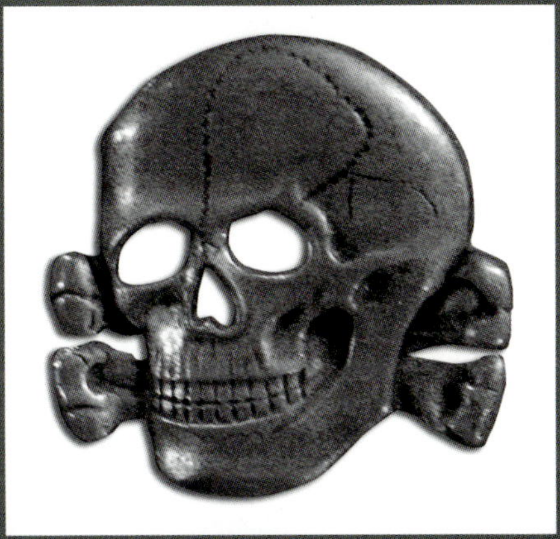

Totenkopf: the death's head.

Introduction

The SS Division Totenkopf, like most Waffen-SS divisions, went through a scrappy evolution before constitution as a full-fledged armored division. Formed in October 1939, mainly from SS concentration camp guards—the SS-Totenkopfverbände—and a sprinkling of SS militia that had seen service in Poland, the division was first commanded by SS-Obergruppenführer Theodor Eicke.

Initially held in reserve during the battle of France, the unit was committed to combat in Belgium on May 16, 1940. Although ultimately victorious in the campaign, the Totenkopf suffered heavy losses, including over 300 officers. The division remained in France for refitting until April 1941.

That month, the division was transferred to the Eastern Front where it took part in Operation *Barbarossa*. It advanced through Lithuania and Latvia and by July had penetrated the Stalin Line, knocking at the gates of Leningrad where, in August, it endured some bitter fighting. During the winter, the Totenkopf Division found itself trapped in the Demyansk Pocket for several months, before managing to break out in April 1942. However, it had lost almost 80 percent of its strength, and was redesignated a battle group—Kampfgruppe Eicke—before being sent to France in October 1942 to lick its wounds. The following month, having taken part in the takeover of Vichy France, the division was allocated a tank battalion—to become the 3rd SS Panzer Regiment—the new divisional name changing to the 3rd SS Panzergrenadier Division Totenkopf.

Georg Schäfer received orders to present himself in Munich to join the Waffen-SS in mid-September 1942, just in time for his 18th birthday. He was assigned to become a panzer radio operator and after training in radio operation and gun loading he was sent to Angoulême, France, where the 3rd SS Panzer Regiment was preparing for deployment:

Norbert Hartmann as a Schütze, helmeted and wearing a rare badge from the Hitlerjugend meeting in Potsdam.

SS-Schütze Norbert Hartmann during training.

Training with the tanks took place day and night. It had to be over quickly as we were badly needed on the Eastern Front. I was surprised to find out that I, along with around 60 of my comrades, would be attending an armored vehicle training camp in the countryside. None of us knew why—or how—we'd been chosen. At the camp, we were trained to use the brand-new heavy tanks they called Tigers. The Tiger was the most modern of all our tanks. Now, I was being taught how to be a gunner—the third role I could fill in a panzer crew. I learned how to shoot the famous 8.8-cm gun mounted on that formidable tank.

A group photo of panzer recruits. Sturmmann Norbert Hartmann is on the far left.

A signed photo of Sturmmann Fritz Fuchs, 7th Company, 3rd SS Panzer Regiment Totenkopf, showing his decorations, including the Panzer Badge.

In Profile:
Sturmmann Fritz Fuchs

December 12, 1924

SS-Schütze Fritz Fuchs in his black uniform. He is wearing the diamond-shaped badge of the Hitlerjugend as well as the sports badge.

The young Fritz Fuchs, far left, with his Panzer III crew.

Soldbuch

10 Gebote

Beurlaubungen über fünf Tage

Erholungsurlaub

Pages from Fritz Fuchs's *Soldbuch* (military ID), including confirmation of the award of the Panzer Badge in Silver.

Norbert Hartmann (center) with two comrades, early on in the war.

Taken in winter on the Eastern Front, this provides a good view of a Panzer III from the 3rd SS Panzer Regiment. There are fuel tanks on the rear of this tank, which belongs to the 2nd Company. On the far left is SS-Schütze Söldner, who provided this picture and others.

To the Eastern Front

In February 1943, after several months of refitting in France, the bulk of the Totenkopf received its deployment order to the Eastern Front, specifically to the Ukraine, in the grips of a bitter winter. The Death's Head Division was to see action at the third battle of Kharkov.

Walter Weber was the gunner in Tank 531, 5th Company, 3rd SS Panzer Regiment. He kept a journal of his experiences. He begins by describing the regiment's transfer from France to the Eastern Front:

> I found myself on the platform at Angoulême train station, in France. The access ramps onto the flatbed wagons had been installed and, to the noise of clanking panzer tracks, we watched the drivers loading our tanks for the trip to Russia and the Eastern Front. Besides the tanks, we had our own packs as well as various crates of matériel. One after the other, our superb tanks were loaded onto the train. We were so proud of our unit.
>
> After the last tank had been loaded, the train moved off. We crossed France, then Germany and Poland, and finally arrived in the Ukraine. The Russian winter was in full swing.

Adolf Suwe and his crew in front of their Panzer III during the winter of 1942/43. The men's names are written along the bottom of the photograph.

Two tankers cranking a Panzer III engine while two more, perched on the hood, have opened the engine hatches.

In Profile:
Unterscharführer Franz Holze

Rottenführer Franz Holze wearing his Ostmedaille and KVK ribbons.

Franz Holze, taken in 1944 before his death in combat later that year.

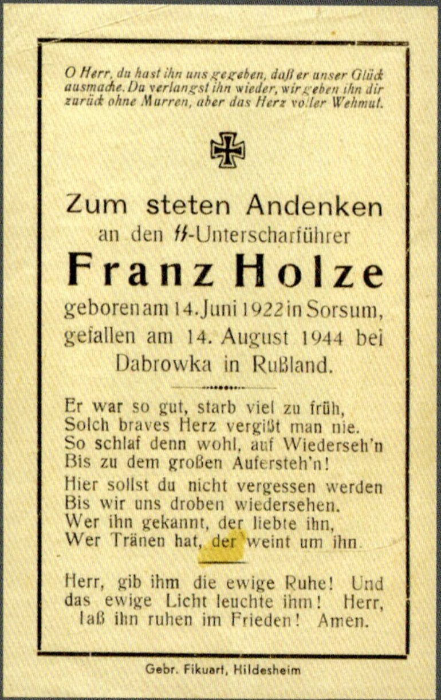

O Herr, du hast ihn uns gegeben, daß er unser Glück ausmache. Du verlangst ihn wieder, wir geben ihn dir zurück ohne Murren, aber das Herz voller Wehmut.

Zum steten Andenken
an den SS-Unterscharführer
Franz Holze
geboren am 14. Juni 1922 in Sorsum,
gefallen am 14. August 1944 bei
Dabrowka in Rußland.

Er war so gut, starb viel zu früh,
Solch braves Herz vergißt man nie.
So schlaf denn wohl, auf Wiederseh'n
Bis zu dem großen Aufersteh'n!
Hier sollst du nicht vergessen werden
Bis wir uns droben wiedersehen.
Wer ihn gekannt, der liebte ihn,
Wer Tränen hat, der weint um ihn.

Herr, gib ihm die ewige Ruhe! Und das ewige Licht leuchte ihm! Herr, laß ihn ruhen im Frieden! Amen.

Gebr. Fikuart, Hildesheim

O Eltern und Geschwister mein!
Ich kehre nicht mehr zu Euch heim.
Mein letzter Gedanke, mein letzter Blick,
Der eilte noch zu Euch zurück.
Mußt' ich so früh von Euch geh'n,
Im Himmel: Auf ein Wiederseh'n!

Unterscharführer Franz Holze's death notice (front and back).

A Totenkopf Panzer III crosses a river, passing a Heer column heading in the opposite direction.

Georg Schäfer served with the Heavy Company, 3rd SS Panzer Regiment Totenkopf, equipped with Panzer VI Tiger Is:

> In December 1942, the Heavy Company was formed, and was loaded onto railway wagons in a convoy headed for Russia. The presence of the new tanks was still a secret, so our Tigers were covered with large canvases. As for us, we bedded down on the straw in our cattle trucks. It was already cold, but it was nothing compared to what we would experience later, when the temperatures would drop below -50°C. There would be a lot of frostbite.
>
> When we arrived at Poltava, we unloaded our tanks and drove towards the front, and our baptism of fire. It was a difficult time for me as it was very cold, and we didn't have any beds to sleep in. The only place we could sleep was inside our tanks. Sometimes, we turned the engine on to get some warmth into the compartment, but it was dangerous to do so as any noise made in Russia was a loud one. Our tank was painted white in winter and brown and green for summer.

Walter Weber recalled arriving on the Eastern Front, and the challenges of the terrain and weather:

> At Poltava, where we offloaded the tanks, we were welcomed with falling snow. Once again, we checked our vehicles. Two days later, we were on our way to the front. We stopped in a small village at the front for the night. The little thatched huts were a first for us, a glimpse of a whole new world that we were about to enter. After camouflaging our tanks, we brought in some food, which we shared with our Ukrainian hosts, who were grateful for it. We had begun our lives as soldiers on the Eastern Front.
>
> One evening, we received orders to deploy. It had been snowing all day, so the road was iced over and dangerous to drive on. The wheels on our vehicles slid more than they rolled, but we managed to advance little by little. Here and

A Panzer III with its crew and some Russian prisoners being transported to a PoW camp.

> there, tanks were lying at the side of the road, having lost control and crashed, now waiting to be rescued by the big half-tracks or other tanks, the crews having long since given up their futile attempts to free their vehicles.
>
> Our tank also ended up in a snowbank and, when we tried to get it out, the left track snapped. But we were still in good spirits, and once the mechanics arrived, it didn't take too long to get it fixed and back on the road. After a few hours, we had rejoined the armored column.
>
> The next day, it rained, rendering the roads impractical in a different way. Faced with the most unspeakable amount of mud, we were again delayed by an accident. A transmission line broke and as our mechanics were still in the rear, we once more had to wait—this time in a Russian village—to be rescued.

Werner Biehl was a mechanic, working in the *Werkstatt*, the repairs and maintenance workshop of the Totenkopf Panzer Regiment. He explains the challenges faced by the workshop that spring as the regiment was advancing east:

> I recall that winter of early 1943 when that the vehicle at the head of the column set a decent pace, and I often had my foot down on the gas. Our long trail of vehicles meandered along the unpaved Russian roads. We had to drive day and night to stay close to the armored combat troops, so we could respond quickly if they needed help. Signs along the muddy, mired "roads" told us not to drive in the deep tracks.
>
> When we were kids, we were lucky to be able to wash in galvanized tubs where our mothers scrubbed us with soap; out here we dreamed of being able to bathe. Sometimes we were so caked in mud that we looked like statues. Some

of the vehicles benefited from large chains to help them cross the rivers of mud, which sometimes contained dead bodies. The color of it was unspeakable, and it was always changing as it was streaked with oil, and it had this peculiar smell. In winter, the mud froze and blocked the vehicles, coating them and hardening like concrete. It was our job to extract them from the frozen quagmires.

Of course, the Russians hadn't built their bridges to support our 60-ton heavy tanks. Some of them collapsed under the weight. Sometimes the tanks would try to drive over the frozen waterways rather than try to cross the bridges. That's what Obersturmführer Rinner tried—he drove his Tiger across a frozen stream, the ice gave way underneath and the tank ended up turret-deep in ice-water! We tried to pull it out onto terra firma with a Bergepanther [an Sd.Kfz. 179 armored personnel carrier], but by the end of the day we'd still had no success.

On February 27 at 0900, Untersturmführer Greisiger received the order to advance. The Bergepanther stayed behind to keep trying to get the Tiger out of the water. It finally succeeded the following day. The "Perebetschino Tiger," as it was nicknamed, had to be towed by four heavy half-tracks, and followed by another to act as a brake, as far as Dnjepropetrovsk, where it could be repaired.

Another of the problems encountered by the repair shops on the front was bands of partisans attacking isolated vehicles, which happened a lot to us as a non-combat unit. In one case, a group of seven men from the repairs unit was caught up in an attack by a group of partisans as large as a company, as well as six T-34s. All the men had to fight back with their rifles, and thanks to the unexpected help of a Heer light Flak section, they managed to escape and return to the workshop. The Speiss made a big fuss, because he thought they had been lost, but the head of the workshop, Untersturmführer Greisiger, sent them back immediately to retrieve the mobile canteen they'd been working on. Luckily it was still there; the partisans hadn't stolen it.

Much of our time was spent at the workshop, taking care of the vehicles that had been brought in for emergency repairs, but we were out in the field a lot, too. Once, a Mercedes truck fell into a huge crater made by an artillery shell. It was transporting a Tiger engine that was expected back at the shop, but was obviously

Hauptsturmführer Walter Bormuth, 1st Battalion, 3rd SS Panzer Regiment Totenkopf.

This Panzer III (R01) has a short 5-cm gun.

Unterscharführer Stanergauk, 3rd SS Panzer Regiment Totenkopf posing proudly in front of his Panzer IV. Stanergauk died on July 5, 1943, during Operation *Citadel*.

An Unterscharführer from 3rd SS Panzer Regiment Totenkopf in the turret of his Panzer III.

delayed! Luckily, there was a heavy truck with a big hoist not far away, so we were able to get the truck out of the hole. But as soon as we solved one problem, there were two more to take its place. The mud bogged down so many vehicles, and we had to get them all out. We were constantly shoveling mud, and it was so exhausting having to dig out tank after tank. We were constantly wet and covered in mud, and it was impossible to make out the shape of our boots underneath it all.

With the help of mechanics like Biehl, Walter Weber's panzer was repaired and:

> By the time the repairs were done, it was nighttime and we resumed our journey by moonlight, behind two other tanks also heading for the front. We didn't have a map, so we just had to follow the other tanks. The first signs of fighting came in the form of the remains of a Soviet munitions supply column that had been utterly destroyed by our troops. Here and there, dead horses and destroyed vehicles, unexploded shells, and ordnance lay scattered across the ground. A light fog veiled the moon.
>
> We stopped at a burning village with not a soul left alive. At the side of the road were three freshly dug graves for our soldiers.
>
> "Forward!" ordered our commander. We continued onward, engines screaming as our vehicles slipped and slithered in the mud in the middle of that vast space, empty and seemingly endless.
>
> We stopped outside another village. A flare appeared in the sky and, as it lit up the surrounding area, we caught a glimpse of two menacing cannons: it was a Flak position. One of the Flak guys approached us, delighted to see the German tanks. We were equally pleased to see him, as it meant we'd already crossed the Russian

lines. A pocket had just formed around Krasnograd and the Soviets there were surrounded.

Heavy snowfall accompanied us on the road that would take us to our first battle. Suddenly, the voice of the company commander came through our headsets, warning us to be on alert and to prepare for combat. We left the main road and turned off onto a track that passed through hilly countryside.

"Keep your eyes open!" barked Ernst, our commander.

The first salutation from the Russians arrived in the form of antitank shells fired from their antitank guns. A very particular feeling came over us at that point, a strange mix of fear and excitement. How were we going to handle ourselves? How were we going to cope? I wished I had a cigarette to calm me. The Russians were firing more and more missiles. A quadruple 2-cm antiaircraft gun carriage not far from us was hit and exploded. The infantry was also suffering losses—death's heavy presence hung in the air.

"Tanks, forward!"

At last, the order had arrived. We showered the enemy with gunfire. Again and again, the Russians tried to stop us with their antitank guns. It didn't work, and they fell back. We were elated that our first attack had gone so well.

The following night, another village was attacked under cover of darkness. Houses were on fire, and lit up the countryside as brightly as if it had been daytime. Slowly, our infantry advanced to the well-fortified village. We supported them as best we could with our tank guns and machine guns, and together we managed to get them into the village.

Adolf Suwe's Panzer III and crewmates in their winter uniforms. The tank has also been given a coat of white paint.

The "first class" carriages used by the Waffen-SS on their train journeys were little more than cattle wagons.

"Tanks, forward!" It was now our turn to enter the village. We were greeted with hellish antitank fire. We were easy targets in the false light, while the enemy was hidden in the darkness. A massive explosion to the left side of our vehicle shook the entire tank. It was a direct hit, so we had to retreat. Slowly and somewhat shakily, we managed to maneuver the tank into a sheltered spot behind a hut. The blow had damaged the track's front guide wheel, breaking several teeth and rendering it basically useless. After the mechanics came and fixed it, we left our shelter to rejoin our company.

In the meantime, the Russians had been slowly retreating from the village, which was now under our control. We camped out on the outskirts, in anticipation of tomorrow's assault. We were able to rest for a while.

The sun rose slowly, accompanied by more snow that was so heavy it effectively blinded us. Our infantry was in front of us, ready to prevent a Soviet counterattack. Suddenly, something moved in front of us: we heard the noise of horses whinnying, of tracks, of engines, and Russian voices. We were stunned and prepared ourselves for the worst, but nothing happened. We couldn't see anything through the curtain of snow. Scouts returned with news of a Russian supply unit passing close by, just meters from where we were lying in wait, hidden even at that range by the snow.

We waited a while, and just as silence returned, the order rang out: "Start your engines; tanks to the fore!" We got into formation, and attacked the Russian

In Profile:

Georg Schäfer

November 9, 1924–February 15, 2002

A rare colorized photograph showing Georg Schäfer wearing the Iron Cross 2nd class ribbon, the Wound Badge and the Panzer Badge.

Georg Schäfer's Tiger, with crew, during Operation *Citadel*. Schäfer is indicated by a drawn-on arrow. The "three bars" symbol is visible on the frontal armor.

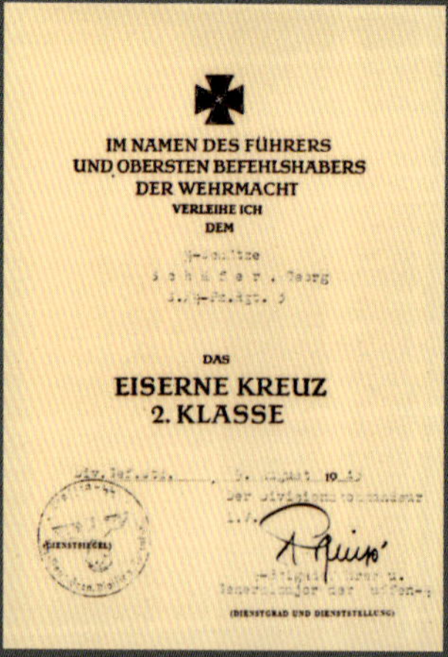

IM NAMEN DES FÜHRERS
UND OBERSTEN BEFEHLSHABERS
DER WEHRMACHT
VERLEIHE ICH
DEM

DAS

EISERNE KREUZ
2. KLASSE

(DIENSTGRAD UND DIENSTSTELLUNG)

The Iron Cross 2nd class certificate awarded to Georg Schäfer.

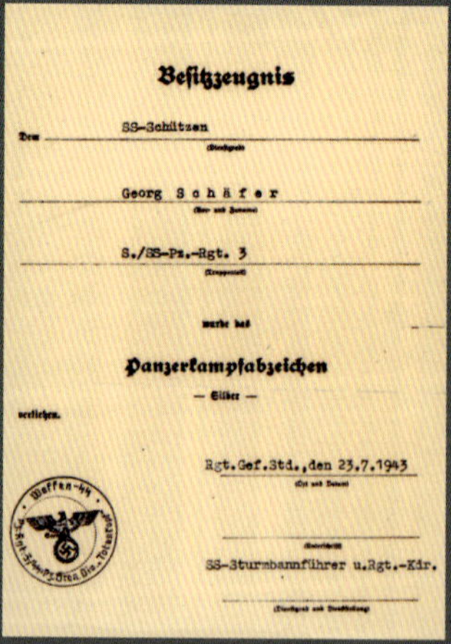

Besitzzeugnis

Dem SS-Schützen

Georg Schäfer

S./SS-Pz.-Rgt. 3

wurde das

Panzerkampfabzeichen

— Silber —

verliehen.

Rgt.Gef.Std.,den 23.7.1943

SS-Sturmbannführer u.Rgt.-Kdr.

The Panzer Badge certificate awarded to Georg Schäfer. Interestingly, it has not been signed.

Georg Schäfer, in camouflage overalls. with one of his comrades.

column. We destroyed it, and tightened the noose on the cauldron a little more, so the Russians were no longer able to set up their antitank guns in decent positions. All that was left were the charred hulks of Soviet artillery and the bodies of Russian soldiers.

A thick fog blanketed the countryside. The trees and the hedges were covered in white. All was silent. The only sign of movement was our guards, patrolling through the snow, fairly high up, keeping an eye on our tanks. Most of our comrades were sleeping, wrapped up in woolen blankets inside the tanks. I got up to stomp some warmth back into my feet as the sun began to peep out from behind the hills. The guards went from tank to tank to wake up the sleeping crews. The commander called the platoon leaders over; our tank commander extricated himself from the tangle of blankets and exited through the turret, launching himself into the snow.

After the commanders' briefing, we were heading into battle yet again. We would be attacking near Kharkov to take the Rogan airfield that supplied the town with food and munitions. The engines started up, reverberating across the snow. The tank tracks sank and slid through the thick snow.

The first Russian infantrymen appeared through the fog, only to disappear again as soon as they spotted us, fleeing back to the nearby village. The first rays of the sun broke through, illuminating the bleached-out silhouettes of the Russians as we arrived outside the village. We shot them down easily, and took the village almost without a fight. We stopped to search the houses and cellars, and took a lot of prisoners, mostly elite Soviet Mongolian troops. We continued our advance and were soon approaching the Rogan airfield. There, too, we did not encounter much resistance, as most of the troops were infantry. The few tanks they had were quickly destroyed, as most of the enemy troops dispersed and fled.

The next village was much more strongly defended. And we had another problem: one of the engine cylinders was jammed, maybe frozen or

A member of the Adolf Suwe's Tiger crew in a type of camouflage known as "peas."

Sturmmann Werner Schünemann (right) with a comrade in camouflage trousers. They look very young indeed.

A Panzer III crew from Waldemar Riefkogel's unit snatches a bite to eat during a lull in the fighting during the Russian winter of 1942/43. Note the three rings around the barrel—the tank's kills.

distorted by the cold. We tried to start the engine with the crank, but without success. We had to wait where we were while the other panzers continued the advance.

Suddenly, a shrill noise heralded a large Russian shell—172 mm—landing close by. We had been spotted and targeted by the Russians. Another shell, this time better aimed, hit the tank. I was wounded in my left hand and hip; my comrade screamed—he'd been hit in the arm—and collapsed on the side of the tank. We radioed for backup. Another tank came to our aid and we were taken to hospital. It was March 13, 1943.

Georg Schäfer remembers the fighting when the regiment first arrived on the Eastern Front:

> Fierce fighting was waiting for us when we arrived at the front. We fought legions of tanks, and I destroyed several T-34s. Sometimes we were on the offensive, sometimes the defensive. We had taken an oath that we would defend Germany and the Führer. We—the Waffen-SS—were nicknamed "the firemen of the Eastern Front," and the Heer units were always happy to see us on their flanks as they knew they could count on us to hold the front. In winter 1942/43, I got to know the muddy roads of Russia. In time I became a tank commander! I wore camouflage overalls, which were also fleeced to keep the cold out.
>
> On one occasion, we had to tow another vehicle; it was lighter than ours but had become bogged down in the mud. As I was going through the necessary maneuvers to extract the tank, I was very surprised to stumble upon an old friend

A 2nd Company Panzer III crew; from left: Steglich, Meinecke, Zimung, and Frommelt. Some Ukrainian children are having a look at the tank—one has even climbed on, June 1943.

from my hometown. We were so far from home, but fate or chance had brought us together again. The atmosphere was very good and we shared our food around. (By an even greater stroke of fate, we met again in 1946, back home!)

That winter, the cold in Russia was intense and we suffered greatly. There was also an outbreak of lice to deal with, not to mention another equally exhausting battle.

March 1943, and spring brought us another ordeal. We had been surrounded near Kharkov and, for the last four weeks, we had been defending ourselves against vicious Russian attacks. The Luftwaffe brought in supplies, but food was always left till last. So, we had also been hungry for four weeks. However, we found a millet factory in our little cauldron that had grain bins full to bursting, and our cooks took full advantage. It was cooked without sauce and without sugar into a kind of porridge, but it was good if you were hungry. Horses that had died and had frozen solid also provided us with a source of food. As water was also in short supply, we weren't able to wash daily and the lice were everywhere. When we were outside in the cold, they weren't too much of a problem, but when we were inside where it was warmer, the little beasts woke up. We scratched every nook and cranny of our tormented bodies.

We were finally rescued by our comrades later in the spring; the front was moving away from us, and the fighting went with it. We also received new recruits to replace the dead and wounded and new vehicles—tanks, trucks, etc.—to replace those destroyed or damaged. Now that things had calmed down, we were able to repair our gear, which had been through a lot, both in terms of cold and combat. Our repair shop had a lot to do. Our vehicles were getting new camouflage, and we had to prepare quickly for a new battle. I felt—we all felt—that something big was about to happen, and not just because our leave had been cancelled.

Hauptsturmführer Richter, wearing his Knight's Cross. During the fighting at Kharkov, he commanded the 5th Company, 3rd SS Panzer Regiment.

Kursk

The battle of Kursk in July 1943 was to be the final strategic offensive that the Germans were able to launch on the Eastern Front. The codename was Operation *Citadel* (*Zitadelle*), an attack aimed at a double envelopment concentrated on Kursk with the principal aim of surrounding the Red Army forces of five armies and closing off the salient. The Germans committed two army groups: Army Group Center, which was to form a northern pincer, and Army Group South, which would launch its powerful panzer divisions, including the Totenkopf, against the southern face of the salient.

In mid-April, 1943, Georg Schäfer found himself on the southern part of the front, near Kharkov, Kursk, Oryol, and Belgorod. He and his comrades were told repeatedly that *Citadel* was delayed, but they had no idea why. "It wasn't until the evening of July 4, 1943 that we were told that the long-awaited offensive was to begin the next day: July 5, 1943."

Wounded on March 13, 1943, Walter Weber spent several weeks in various hospitals then rejoined his unit near Kharkov in the spring. He recalled they were champing at the bit to get back to the front, it was a long wait and the men became very impatient. Eventually the call came:

> We were put on high alert for an offensive on Belgorod, and on the evening of the first day we moved out, leaving nothing but dust. We had no idea what we were doing at that time. The next day, we arrived in a forest, where we stayed until evening. Then we started moving again. The day after that, just before midday, we reached our target, another forest where we camouflaged ourselves until the attack. Our

Hauptsturmführer Richter wearing his Knight's Cross. At Kursk he commanded the Heavy Panzer (Tiger) Company, 3rd SS Panzer Regiment.

Two members of a Tiger crew from Georg Schäfer's Heavy Company relax with a couple of bottles of wine.

> Spiess checked all the equipment again and then took the roll call. We weren't far from the front, but we couldn't hear anything much from that direction—just Soviet reconnaissance planes flying overhead, which our Flak took care of in short order.
>
> On the evening of July 3, 1943, we had a little party; it was the last party that a lot of those men would ever have.

Schäfer details how, when his company arrived at their start position, it was covered with barbed wire and deminers' flags:

> The message was clear: we would have to stick fastidiously to the marked-out pathways. We were sure the pathfinders had done a great job and, as the infantry were waiting for our support, we had to cross the minefield. And anyway, we had been told that our Tigers were basically immune to mines, so what did we have to worry about? As soon as we received the order, our 51 heavy Tigers prepared to cross the minefield. I ordered my driver to move forward, and the others to follow me. I sealed my turret and glued myself to my periscopes.
>
> Mines detonated under our tracks, barely registering inside the tank. It made us complacent, though, and it wasn't long before a massive explosion threw us violently against the walls of the compartment. The Tiger reared up like a startled horse and slammed back down with a loud thud. I suspected one of the tracks was in bad shape. We were in the middle of the minefield, so there was no way we were going to get out and check them! Instead, I used the radio to call the pathfinders, and asked them to come and clear the area around the tank. Next, I called our repairs shop and asked them to send a vehicle out to get the tank started again, and to fix any damage. They did, and the mechanics were able to get the old girl

going again. The pathfinders told me that we had driven over a big American-made mine that had left a crater over a meter wide and a meter deep.

With the repairs made, I radioed my company to let them know we were on our way back. That was easier said than done, as we had a number of obstacles still to overcome, like a big antitank ditch. I got out of the tank to guide the driver, and when we'd made it over, I signaled to him to stop at the next hillock on the right, where I could get back into my turret. Around 1,200–1,500 meters to the left, the Russians were waiting for us. As I was climbing back into the tank, we took a direct hit, and I was wounded in the back of my head.

That was the end of Schäfer's battle, and his service with the regiment. He was in a coma for four weeks, and woke temporarily blind and unable to speak. He only left hospital in September 1943, joining the ersatz battalion [replacement battalion] at Beneschau, not far from Prague. There he was awarded the Iron Cross 2nd class, the Panzer Badge in Silver for 12 days in combat with a tank, and the Wound Badge (Verwundetenabzeichen). He was then sent to Riga, where another armored unit, the SS-Sturmgeschütz Battalion 16 RFSS, was being formed. "I became part of it and soon found myself in Italy without my brave Tiger. I would be seriously injured in combat in Hungary on March 9, 1945 with this unit, losing part of my right leg and all my crew. If I had my Tiger, maybe things would have been different. But who knows—that's life, huh?"

Weber recalled the beginning of the *Citadel* offensive:

On July 4, just before nightfall, we formed up into our assault positions. The night of July 4/5, 1943, was clear and starry. Artillery thundered over the horizon and tracers streaked across the sky like lightning. A Soviet artillery bombardment illuminated what was about to become the stage for one of the biggest offensives in the East. Artillery fire from both sides was like a call and response.

Three Unterscharführer panzer crew sit on the frontal armor plating of their Tiger. Its 8.8-cm gun and almost invincible armor made it a much-feared machine.

In Profile: Panzers

The Waffen-SS was always first in the queue when it came to tanks, and the 3rd SS Panzer Regiment was no exception, even receiving some new Tigers in the last week of the war, in May 1945. Evolving from the earlier Panzer III, the mainstay of the panzer divisions was the ubiquitous, and highly successful, Panzer IV, with the powerful Panther and imposing Tiger (I and II) becoming more and more common as 1944 unfolded.

A Totenkopf Panzer III during Operation *Citadel.* Note the three-bar insignia on the front of the vehicle.

A brand-new Tiger tank being delivered to the 3rd SS Panzer Division Totenkopf.

A sharp photo of a Tiger (Tank 914), Heavy Company, 3rd SS Panzer Regiment Totenkopf.

An excellent frontal view of a Panzer IV from the 3rd SS Panzer Regiment Totenkopf crossing a bridge. Note that it only has *schürzen* on the turret, the sides' most likely lost. There are a few pieces of track on the glacis, an indication that track repairs have been made.

Three Panzer IVs from the 7th Company. A crew is hard at work refueling and making repairs to the tank on the right (note the gas can).

Above: Kurt Söhrmann's Panther (with furniture piled on the back) on the journey through Poland, seen here at Okumin in 1944.

Left: Ernst Walter Kirsch (under the X) on his Panther during transportation to the front.

We drove for a few hours and reached the frontline, and prepared for H-hour. Our artillery continued to roar overhead, pounding Russian positions. Nebelwerfers filled the sky with their white smoke. We were in our jump-off positions when the sun started to rise, revealing an incredible scene.

I had never seen so many mechanized forces gathered together in one place. It was like something from Dante. Heavy and light vehicles, supported by newly replenished artillery, all ready for what we know knew was going to be a decisive battle in the East. A multitude of troops were ready and waiting for their starting orders, to crush the enemy and roll back the front.

Aviation was just as active as the ground forces. Squadrons of Stukas roared above us, one after the other, escorted by fighters. Then the Russian dive-bombers appeared, and we were ordered to dig in to reduce the effect of the bombs and minimize casualties. We were so busy digging that we didn't hear a squadron of Russian bombers flying directly overhead. By the time we heard the whistling of the bombs, the first ones were already exploding, and it was too late.

The force of the explosions cracked the armor on our tanks, and turned the horizons yellow. The air was filled with smoke and dust from the bombs and shells, and the armored vehicles. The wounded screamed and called out help. As the air started to clear and become breathable again, we could make out the burning wreck of a tank, with the dead and wounded scattered all around. A few injured men tried to crawl away from the burning tank, as we called for the medics. One of our crew, who had tried to take cover under the tank, had been hit by shrapnel. His body was torn apart; there was nothing we could do for him.

Another Tiger, this one coated in *zimmerit*. The soldier pictured took his accordion everywhere.

Two Tigers from the Heavy Company of the Panzer Regiment Totenkopf. The tank in the foreground is number 922, and the three vertical bars of the division are visible on the frontal armor plating of both vehicles.

We had to use almost all of our reserves to reform our tank crews. Our Flak was hard at work, and we rejoiced when we saw an enemy aircraft going down in flames and crashing into the ground in an explosion of fire and flame. We saw a few parachutes deploy, and commandos were immediately sent out to bring back the survivors.

Around 1500, we finally set off. The first wave had already advanced and were pushing back the first Soviet defenses, which were very well organized and strongly defended. Our tank hit one of hundreds of mines that the Russians had laid, so we were stuck—again!—waiting for the mechanics. The crew inspected the tank to assess the damage; nothing major, but it did delay us. We spent the night there, camping in a field.

The next morning, we were woken by heavy rain. It was still dark and, to save ourselves from getting soaked through, we took refuge under the tank. But our troubles didn't end there: before the sun had even risen, a light Soviet bomber decided to use us as target practice. Thankfully, he wasn't very good. At last, the sky to the east began to brighten, the rain stopped, and we left our cover to wait patiently for new orders.

The orders came through: to cross the Donets River and destroy the Soviet defenses on the other side. As the sun started to rise, we headed toward the river. A mist coming off the Donets made it tough to identify the Soviet defenses, but we could make out the soon-to-be battlefield. Suddenly, a hail of antitank shells and mortars came from the opposite bank. Every Russian gun was firing at us, but we had no idea where from or how to respond. The sun was behind us so we were a perfect target. The best we could do was to throw some smoke grenades and withdraw into a small wood, which at least prevented us from losing too many men.

In Profile:
Panzer III

A 5th Company Panzer III, mounted with 5-cm long-barreled gun. This was commander Adolf Suwe's tank. This type of panzer had already been updated by 1943 but was always a solid addition to a panzer regiment. The gray paint is tired; also note the replacement wheels on the back of the tank.

A sharp head-on image of a Totenkopf Panzer III taking a breather in the lee of a Ukrainian *izba* during the Kursk offensive, Operation *Citadel*. Note the extended signals aerial.

An excellent photo of a 3rd SS Panzer Regiment Panzer III. Norbert Altmann first saw service in this vehicle.

A few hours later, we were ordered to head to a village behind the wood, but we were targeted by Russian fighter-bombers. After cleaning our guns and readying the tank for further battle, we took some time out to prepare ourselves. The cook served up some chicken noodle soup, a delicacy I'm sure we would remember for a long time, as our supplies were starting to run low.

While we were enjoying the soup, an infantryman came running towards us, shouting, "The Russian tanks are coming!" We dropped everything and clambered quickly into our tank, our tank commander soon following the company commander to counter the enemy. A report came in from the staff informing us that a Soviet attack had broken through and enemy soldiers were now in our sector. Around 500 to 600 meters from the village, we found a place to await the enemy attack. Several times, we were alerted to the presence of tanks nearby, but nothing happened. It was frustrating. I cursed that infantryman for making me trade my chicken soup for this interminable waiting.

As quiet as it was for us, in the village it was a ruckus. Russian tanks were somewhere in the vicinity, firing on it like crazy. All of a sudden, I snapped out of my stupor, as I heard the sound of tank tracks coming from the top of a nearby hill. It was a Russian tank, but it didn't seem to have spotted us. When it was about 200 meters away, I fired an antitank shell at it from our long 5-cm gun—our Panzer III was armed with a 5-cm KwK 39 L/60. The shell ricocheted off the thick armor in front of the turret and bounced with a flash off into the sky. Other tanks also fired at the enemy tank, but with the same results, until a Marder III hit it with a 75-mm shell, which destroyed it completely. A T-34 rushed us at full speed, and at 50 meters I fired a shell at its engine. It kept coming for a couple of seconds, on fire, but it was done for.

A Tiger from the Heavy Company of the SS Panzer Division Totenkopf. Note the lack of *zimmerit* and the shovel on the glacis. This is Untersturmführer Kössler's Tiger 911.

A half-track *Zugmaschine* (lit. motor tractor) from the repairs and maintenance unit in front a Heavy Company Tiger—Unterscharführer Lachner's—which is being repaired in the shelter of some trees following mechanical problems. Note the insignia and small "s" (for *schwere:* heavy) on the mudguard of the half-track.

The other tanks in the company were fighting the Russians too. Apparently, we'd completely surprised the enemy. They were all over the place, and didn't seem to be following any orders, shooting while moving, which made it very difficult to hit anything.

An English Churchill I [Lend-Lease] was coming toward us; at 40, maybe 50 meters, I fired a shell that struck it between its turret and armor plating. The crew stopped the tank and jumped out in short order, before taking cover in the long grass. So far, two waves of Soviet tanks had attacked us without making any impression and it looked like we were going to have a short respite. The remains of destroyed Soviet tanks dotted the battlefield.

All too soon a third wave started coming down from the top of the hill. I had positioned the turret at ten o'clock, maybe a little more to the left, when the driver shouted, "Russian tank ahead!" And in that moment, I froze. Masked behind the Churchill that I had just destroyed, another Churchill had been approaching us—and it was now just 20 meters from us. Why it didn't fire at us, I'll never know. In any event, I did fire, and hit it straight on, piercing its frontal armor. Two of the crew managed to escape, and our machine gun took care of the third.

That was the last tank of the assault; eleven lay as burned-out hulks in front of us. On our side, one of our tanks had been hit by a shell and another had been rammed by a T-34 in a suicide attack, but miraculously we hadn't lost any men.

We headed to the village, where many of the rear-echelon troops had fled in the panic, but not our brave cook, who had stayed put in case anyone came back for his chicken noodle soup. Unfortunately for him—and us—we didn't have much time for food, as another fight was in the offing.

During the night, infantrymen arrived to secure the area and support our armored unit. We were thankful, as they helped us wipe out a Russian infantry attack as well as the light T-70 tank supporting it. The glow from the still-smoldering wrecked tanks helped us, but also helped the Russian fighter-bombers that were out to make us pay for the losses we'd inflicted on them earlier.

At first light the next day, we examined the battlefield. Littered among the tank carcasses were charred bodies, dead and wounded. It was a gruesome sight.

Other companies were arriving to join us for the advance. Our company commander greeted the regimental commander as the latter drove by in his armored car, thanking us for the previous day's victory with a wave of his hand. That raised our spirits and we felt good as we prepared for the next fight.

It was less violent than the day before. Despite advancing without too much opposition, we received the order to stop. We got into hedgehog formation in a field, awaiting further orders, before withdrawing into the cover of a small wooded area. We took the opportunity to clean our weapons, freshen up, and to eat something. The night was punctuated by frequent appearances of light bombers dropping bombs and randomly strafing our positions to keep us on our toes. These little "mosquitos" came one after the other, dropping parachutes flares to locate us, the flares exuding an eerie yellow glow.

A sharp image of a Panzer III used by commanders of the 3rd SS Panzer Regiment during Operation *Citadel*. Made of wood, the gun is artificial to make space for signals equipment. Note the three-bar insignia on the front left mudflap.

Obersturmführer Lummitsch (with pipe) and Oberscharführer Swetlie on the turret of their Panzer III, with their German shepherd, during Operation *Citadel*. They are part of the reconnaissance platoon (Aufklarungs. Zug) of the Staff Company, 1st Battalion, 3rd SS Panzer Regiment.

We stayed in the wood until the following afternoon, when we received the order to continue the advance. At the end of the day we pitched our tents in the pouring rain, to rest up and to try and sleep before another day of fighting.

"Platoon leaders, report to the company commander!" That was our wake-up call. We barely had time for our morning ablutions and a quick breakfast, as we knew that we would soon be on our way again. When they returned, our platoon leaders ordered us to get ready as quickly as possible because we had new objectives. In this sector too, the Russians tried to break through, but here too, it ended badly for them. We even managed to capture some of their tanks intact. We immediately turned them against their former owners, but now daubed with big black crosses.

Around midday, we attacked again, and were welcomed by heavy antitank and artillery fire. We noticed some new vehicles arriving off to the side, dropping off infantrymen right next to us. The antitank barrage intensified. One of our tanks was destroyed and others were hit. Some of the crewmembers were wounded and had to be evacuated and replaced. Slowly, we advanced. Part of our company stayed back as a rearguard. We continued our attack, progressing up a shallow gully, then slowing down to catch our breath and let the infantry catch up.

The infantry signaled that there were some well-camouflaged Russian tanks ahead of us. We braced ourselves before pushing on. Antitank shells rained down for what seemed like hours, but they were too high and passed clear over us.

In the evening, we approached the next village and captured it with all guns blazing. There wasn't a Soviet tank in sight. Houses and trucks that had been respectively storing and transporting munitions were in flames, exploding in huge bursts of pyrotechnics, just like it was Walpurgis Night. Then the enemy bombers arrived, making use of the light to target us with a deluge of bombs. The earth heaved, and we were shaken inside our tanks, suffering too from the flames and the smoke. The noise of the bombs was close to unbearable, deafening us not just with their explosions but with the shrapnel hitting the sides of the tanks, and with the reverberations they caused.

After the third attack, we departed the sector and regrouped in a gully where we rested a little before another day of fighting. It was a clear night and all the stars were out. A light, warm wind swept across the fields. After almost 14 hours of uninterrupted combat, we returned to our positions a little calmer, hoping to catch a bit of sleep. At midnight, it was my turn to stand watch, and I patrolled among the tanks, smoking one cigarette after another to keep awake.

The Russian bombers found us again. They dropped illuminating parachute flares, followed by real bombs. At 0200 I was finally relieved. I bundled myself up under our tank and had just dropped off to sleep when a shout woke me: "Prepare ammunition!" I hit the ground running. It was 0300. There was a lot to do before daybreak—cleaning and checking weapons, grabbing some breakfast—so there was no chance of getting back to sleep. I wouldn't have been able to anyway what with all the noise of the Russian antitank guns. When our weapons were ready, we curled up in our tanks with some food and waited for orders.

At one point we heard someone shouting. A Russian shell had killed one man and wounded two more. We continued to eat our breakfast. Then, suddenly, it was all go: the platoon commander set off and we followed him, getting our tank in order as we went. We hadn't gone more than 100 meters across a field before we spotted a group of T-34s ahead of us.

The company command post during Operation *Citadel*. Behind the amphibious Schwimmwagen is a Panzer III, bedecked with crewmembers' helmets and a layer of straw for camouflage.

Two sidecars and an Opel Blitz, all bearing the three-bar insignia of the division, during Operation *Citadel.* In the background are Totenkopf panzers.

They charged at us with all the power their diesel engines could muster. We halted and began to fire. The first few tanks erupted in flame; the others continued, focused on keeping their course—straight for us! One of them reached our tank, but we managed to avoid it thanks to some deft maneuvering by our driver. The T-34 was hit several times by our comrades, and the noise of the explosion that followed was deafening.

Two other T-34s tried to ram us. I took out the one on the right with two shells, but the one on the left kept coming. It was finally stopped by one of the other tanks in our platoon. Little by little, one after the other, all the Soviet tanks were destroyed and there was nothing left but burning carcasses over the battlefield.

I destroyed a third tank that day. It was turning around in front of us, trying to escape, so I shot its engine and blew it up. When all the tanks were destroyed, the Russian infantry attacked. It was so absurd; I've never seen anything like it. They came at us shoulder-to-shoulder, in waves, with nothing but their rifles and bayonets! Our guns and machine guns made mincemeat of them. We crushed a heavy machine-gun team under our tracks, leaving a bloody smear on the ground. We had no problem eliminating them, though some of them did get quite close to our own infantrymen. Solid fire kept them off, though.

Suddenly, we were subjected to renewed and intensified antitank fire. Shells banged on the sides of our tank—three direct hits on one side of our Panzer III, but the armor remained intact. Luckily, they were 47 mm and we took care of the offending piece with our 5 cm. Each time we were hit, everything in the tank went flying. Then the engine stopped.

A lot of our tanks had been hit, and we'd all got bogged down. Another panzer towed us out of the mud, but an enemy shell had smashed the cooling fan. The field mechanics couldn't fix it so we had to be towed back to the company workshop.

I returned to the company as quickly as I could, but everything had calmed down. We were discussing calling in replacements and getting some rest while things were quiet, but we suspected it was the calm before the storm and decided to stay at the front.

Soon enough, we heard the sound of tank tracks from an armored unit on the move coming from behind a nearby hill. A Luftwaffe Henschel reconnaissance aircraft flew over the enemy and sent us their coordinates, but the Soviets didn't show themselves.

That evening, we withdrew about 25 kilometers. The next day, after a quiet night, the three of us cleaned our weapons and answered the morning roll call. We were then called in front of the company commander: he awarded us the Iron Class 2nd class [Eisernes Kreuz 2 Klasse] and shook hands firmly with each of us. Returning to our positions, we finished up with cleaning the weapons, ready for combat.

Unterscharführer Stettner was a panzer commander in 5th Company, commanded by Hauptsturmführer Flohr during Operation *Citadel:*

After crossing the antitank ditches, we regrouped into a formation with our company at the head, and Obersturmführer Westphal and his 6th Company to our left. We skirted a valley and arrived at a rise. A vast, flat plain of grassland rolled out ahead of us. Beyond that was the Donets valley. Some distance in front of us was a village that, according to our map, was called Nepohajewo. We could only see the roofs, though. Just behind the village was a small forest. Suddenly, flashes of light started emanating from the village; we were being targeted by antitank guns. We responded, and our artillery took the village under fire. The Russian guns responded, and large shells started falling among our tanks. It was such a bombardment that to continue resisting would have been suicide. We were ordered to fire smoke cannisters, which provided cover for a retreat. Shrapnel from a large Russian shell damaged my front left drive wheel. I relayed the problem to the platoon leader, Obersturmführer Burgschulte. The Russian fire diminished, with only a few shells falling here and there. We returned to the village of Smorodino, where were went to the repair shop, who had been notified of our arrival. Elements from the SPW Battalion [mechanized infantry] took over the attack.

While we were still occupied at the workshop, a reconnaissance plane flew overhead, sending up a purple flare to let us know that an armored force was approaching fast. Our 5th Company, which had taken cover in the village, went out to meet the assailants. A little while later, the panzergrenadiers reappeared at the top of the hill, covered by the fire of the SPW. Holding the village was going to be impossible. Suddenly, a vehicle pulled up fast and braked hard beside us. The Speiss, Hauptscharführer Diegusch, shouted at us to mount up and evacuate. I clambered into my tank and grabbed the frequency codes, rendering the radio useless, before jumping into the Speiss's truck alongside my crewmates. We crossed the village, small-arms fire erupting around us. Our tanks were counterattacking.

The next day, our company, under Hauptsturmführer Flohr, attacked on the left, towards Veselyy. Accompanied by an artillery observation tank, we passed through a valley via a village, and reached Hill 224.5. To my left was Uzelino's Panzer III, and to my right, Untersturmführer Burgschulte's. We were in formation at the top of the hill; in front of us, a large open slope led down into another valley. Around 500 meters straight ahead of us was a group of T-34s. We opened fire on them immediately. Uzelino fired and hit a T-34 with his first shot. Some way to the right, another T-34 caught fire. Suddenly, Uzelino left formation; we thought he'd gone mad, until we saw the entire crew climbing out of the tank and sheltering behind it. Then all hell broke loose. Flak fire came from the left, antitank fire from the right. Through my headset, I heard the gunner saying that the firing pin was unserviceable. Then came an order from the commander to head for cover. However, I didn't want to leave Uzelino and his crew to the Russians. I told the driver to head full-speed for Uzelino, as another shell hit their tank. We hoisted the three wounded crewmembers aboard the tank; Uzelino and his loader were uninjured, so they followed close behind. The Russia fire then focused on us as the rest of the company was already safely behind the hill. A piece of the *schürzen* from our left track went flying into the air having been hit by a Russian shell. I swerved to the left, then the right, hoping a zigzag would prevent the Russians from getting a clear shot at us. A shell whizzed past the left side of the turret; there was a bang, and the storage trunk from the back of the turret flew off. Bullets whistled past my head whenever I poked my head out of the turret to check on the wounded. Finally, we reached the top of the hill, and handed the wounded over to some nurses. Uzelino and his loader arrived unscathed.

A Panzer III from the 3rd SS Panzer Division Totenkopf bearing the three-bar insignia adopted by the division for Operation *Citadel*. Note the *schürzen* and the excellent camouflage.

> With our firing pin finally replaced, we rejoined the company and found we had new orders from Hauptsturmführer Flohr. We had to conduct a flanking attack against the village of Kotschetowka. We arrived at the village via a small valley. I stopped the tanks and took my MP 40 to recce the situation. It was not good—five brand-new, factory-fresh T-34s were waiting for us in the woods. The company commander's Kübel appeared, and, with it, the artillery VB [*vorgeschobener beobachter*, the forward observer]. Coordinates were sent back immediately and soon several salvos arrived … beyond the tanks. A quick correction, and the next wave landed right on target.
>
> We went back to our position and decided to take the village. When we entered, we found a large number of tanks and other armored vehicles. Our 16 guns gave them everything they had. As the village was in a valley and surrounded by marshland, there were only two or three escape routes. This worked to our advantage: the VB took the opportunity to send out the coordinates so would-be escapees could be taken out with 10.5-cm shells.

The fighting on July 9/10 1943 cost the Russians a lot of tanks. At 0930 on July 12, the Soviet 5th Guards Tank Army, with 850 tanks and an array of assault guns, attacked the II SS Panzer Corps. Hauptsturmführer Biermeier and his armored group arrived at Hill 226.6 to attack northeast. Stettner continues:

> We had just left when a wave of T-34s rushed us at full speed. They were 100 meters from us, then 50 meters. The gunner shouted that he had one in his sights. He fired, and there was a huge bang that made even our own tank shake. Nothing was left of the T-34 but a few bits of debris, and the wheels flying through the air. It was impossible that our gun alone had done it—they must have had explosives on board. The pathfinders in front of us suffered heavy losses; they fought the T-34s with their hollow charges and destroyed a decent number of them, but there was nowhere for them to hide and protect themselves. Many of the pathfinders were killed by pieces of the tanks they had just destroyed and by shrapnel. The 1st Battalion, 3rd SS Panzer Regiment Totenkopf advanced, and we—the 2nd Battalion—followed soon after. We were ordered up the right flank to help the 1st Company, who'd been blocked by a barrage of antitank guns. Several of their tanks had already been hit. We gave them a helping hand, in particular protecting my friend Heinz Prenzel's damaged tank, until the infantry arrived to relieve us. Then we returned to our positions.
>
> Another tank was retreating and, once in cover, the loader and driver climbed out, carrying the bodies of their commander and radio operator, both of whom had been killed when a shell punched through the armor and into the tank. The surviving crew approached the command post to find a new commander and radio operator. The wounded were treated, but wouldn't leave the front and abandon their comrades.
>
> At 0950, the command post reported over the radio: "The Russians are attacking Wassilijewka," then five minutes later, "The Russians coming from Michailowka are attacking toward the west, with tanks. They want to split the division at the Psel River and surround it. They are in contact with the 2nd and 3rd Battalions of the Eicke Regiment." At 1100, "the Russians have been repelled and chased back to their starting positions."
>
> The 2nd Battalion attacked in broad formation. Just at the extremity of the range of our guns, we spotted the Russian tanks. Suddenly, on my left, one of our

In Profile: Leave

Waffen-SS members were given leave, even on the Eastern Front. Schäfer mentions getting two weeks' leave and Stettner 21 days, in 1944. At the same time, any leave due could be summarily cancelled if an offensive was in the offing. Leave for a Waffen-SS trooper was often fraught: accounts vary as to whether his leave officially began on the Eastern Front, or at home, in Germany. For a start, he faced a hazardous train journey back to Germany, often dealing with attacks by Russian partisans or Soviet "Jabos" dive-bombing and strafing the train. Once home in Germany, particularly if he came from a city, like Berlin, Hamburg or Düsseldorf, he might endure Allied bombing raids, loss of loved ones or even the destruction of the family home, as well as food shortages. Then, all too soon, it was over and he was back on the Eastern Front.

Above and top left: Oberscharführer on leave spending time with his family. The photograph shows his decorations and Totenkopf armband.

Sturmmann Herbert Wrase from the 3rd SS Panzer Regiment Totenkopf with his fiancée.

A Rottenführer from 3rd SS Panzer Regiment Totenkopf on his wedding day. He is wearing his black uniform for the occasion.

The Oberscharführer and his wife share a bottle with a member of the Wehrmacht, perhaps a relative.

An unidentified Rottenführer gets married, on October 23, 1943.

A well-decorated Oberscharführer from the 3rd SS Panzer Regiment on leave in the countryside with his parents and sister.

tanks shuddered and burst into flames. The crew evacuated, under Russian fire. It was then that we realized that we had driven right into a Russian infantry position, the soldiers well camouflaged in the rye fields. Grenades and Molotov cocktails flew through the air. We retreated in a hurry to extricate ourselves from the trap. My comrades to the left and right had disengaged, waiting for the arrival of our infantry, so I asked them to cover me while I tried to clear some of the Russians. My loader, Sturmmann Faber, prepared some M39 grenades. Our panzer edged forward, until we arrived in front of a Russian machine-gun position. Faber handed me two grenades with the pins already removed; I threw them through the open turret into the machine-gun nest. There were two explosions, then the enemy machine gun was silent. We repeated the maneuver several times, with similar success, and managed to clear the area; the few who tried to escape were gunned down by our panzergrenadiers, who had just arrived.

By 1500, our armored group was two kilometers northwest of Poleshajew. By evening, the Russian tanks seemed to have disappeared. In front of us stretched a vast, undulating plain with fields of rye. Suddenly, geysers of earth and fire erupted around us. Those damned heavy antitanks had targeted us. We were trying to get out of their range when a shell hit the ground just in front of us and threw us on top of each other inside the tank. A shower of debris covered the turret. The panzer stopped; but there was no sign of smoke in the tank, at least. The gunner, Rottenführer Ahl, shouted: "We've been hit, everybody out!" I ordered everyone to stay where they were—outside was a storm of fire and steel, far more dangerous.

Hüttinger, the driver, came into view under the gun. His face was contorted. "My legs! My legs!" he moaned. I asked him, "Can you still feel them?" After a pause, he said, "Yes." I told him to get back to his position and get us out of there.

The vastness of the steppes, during the battle of Kursk.

A staff Schwimmwagen from the 3rd SS Panzer Regiment Totenkopf during Operation *Citadel.* The corn field stretches to the horizon. The muzzle of a 5-cm Panzer III gun barrel can just be seen in the bottom left-hand corner.

Hüttinger was just 18 but he managed to control himself and get back into his seat despite the pain. The engine was still operational, and Hüttinger managed to get us turned around. After about 50 meters, I spotted a Panzer IV from the 6th Company firing everything it had at the Russians. I took cover behind him so I could get out and assess the situation to find out what exactly had happened. I could see that the antitank shell had struck at the thickest point of the armor, and had hit the spare pieces of track we'd attached as armor reinforcement. It had worked at least: the shell hadn't blown through into the compartment, though small steel splinters had penetrated, and these were what had injured our driver. It wasn't too serious, though in the heat of the action we'd all been worried it was much worse, and Hüttinger was well enough to keep going.

Our regiment had stumbled into a huge antitank barrage that was only neutralized after a lengthy contest. We were on our way again, and passed one of our tanks that had been destroyed by the Russians, as well as several destroyed enemy antitank guns and the bodies of Russian gunners killed at their posts or thrown farther afield by our artillery. Our attack continued.

The next day [July 13], we found ourselves facing well-concealed Russian infantry positions. In an effort to stop us, Soviet artillery fired on its own troops. We pulled back 200 meters to turn and take the Russian position from the right flank. Suddenly, through our headsets, Hauptsturmführer Flohr ordered us to regroup, and follow the red flares, to press the attack. As usual with Waffen-SS officers, he was at the head of the assault. When we reached the top of a rise, the regiment spread out to attack. From here, we could already see the Russians shooting at us. High-explosive shells at 1,230, 500 meters … Fire! More shots from the Russian side. My gunner spotted an antitank gun, and before I knew it his shell was on its way. It hit its mark and exploded, throwing debris—including a few

Russians—over the surrounding area. Shell after shell followed at a tremendous pace and with phenomenal precision. Before long, the nest of antitank guns had been obliterated. A column of Russian vehicles was fleeing up a valley, but was caught in our fire and disappeared into the thick smoke. On a hill to our right, one kilometer northwest of Poleshajew, stood the rest of our armored regiment. We had lost a few armored vehicles, and it was now 2000, but Flohr ordered: "Follow me, we'll take them from the flank!" At 2245, we reached and secured the road between Beregowoje and Kartaschewka, north of Belgorod, where we set up camp for the night. Our offensive had been a success.

The next day, July 14, at 1730, 3rd SS Panzer Regiment Totenkopf reserves were deployed behind Hill 226.6 and we attacked again, destroying dozens of T-34s. But we paid a high price, losing all ten Tigers, 12 Panzer IVs, one short-barreled Panzer IV, 21 Panzer IIIs and two command panzers. Thanks to the tremendous work by the workshops, many of the vehicles, including several Tigers, were later repaired.

A Totenkopf Panzer III during Operation *Citadel*, with the three-bar insignia of the unit for the operation (only two are visible). It also has nine rings around the gun barrel, one for each of its kills.

Walter Mattern while still a *Junker* (officer cadet) in the Totenkopf Division.

The Mius Front

Following the massive battles in the Kursk salient—the largest the world had ever witnessed—the Soviet Southern Front turned its attention to the Mius Front, the Wehrmacht's three defensive lines. In what was termed the Donbass Strategic Offensive, the Red Army finally penetrated the Mius Front in August 1943 in Rostov Oblast.

Walter Weber describes how after a few days in bivouac, his unit joined the rail convoy to Kharkov. "We were already familiar with the city from earlier that year and the first of the big fights there [the third battle of Kharkov]. We were also familiar with the Mius River, having clashed with the Soviets when they had established a bridgehead there." He recalled that news from the front was not good. After arriving at Stalino (Donetsk), they exchanged their "battered Panzer IIIs for Panzer IVs with the long 7.5-cm gun. It was sad to say goodbye to our brave old girl—we'd already removed all our matériel and personal effects—but that's the way it was." The Panzers IVs were new to them, but had already seen action with the 1st SS Panzer Division Leibstandarte Adolf Hitler.

> The next morning, we drove to our jump-off point for a new attack. Honestly, I had mixed feelings about it, as only three of our company's tanks had made it there. The others had either broken down or, in one case, actually caught fire! The other companies were already there, well-hidden and ready for the attack the next day.

After their woeful experience on the road, five more of our tanks finally arrived during the night. We were positioned quite high up, which we weren't very happy about. Also, the quantity of arms and ammunition arranged for this new offensive made us feel a little uncomfortable, as it wouldn't get us very far. The plan was that the battle would take around ten hours, at the end of which we would destroy the Soviet bridgehead, and then be relieved, and sent back to Germany. I didn't believe it—they were just words, after all, and who knew what might happen—but I hoped, all the same.

A red sun rose in the sky, and silence fell over the front. The infantry arrived and climbed onto our tanks, ready for the attack, which would commence at 0900. The Russians started firing a few shells, which fell here and there but nowhere near us. We drank some coffee as we watched the shells fall harmlessly in no-man's land. Soon, our artillery responded, making so much noise that it temporarily deafened me as I made my preparations in the new tank, and we began to slowly advance.

Two tanks alongside ours stopped suddenly in a cloud of dust. The crew climbed out. After the dust had cleared, we saw the cause of the disruption—a multitude of mines, both buried and lying on the ground, lay in front of us. The infantrymen climbed down and the advance stopped. Pathfinders were quickly summoned to demine the terrain, as Soviet antitank and artillery fire intensified. We were on tenterhooks in our tanks as we waited for ground to be cleared. The hum of Soviet ground-attack aircraft—Ilyushin Il-2 Shturmoviks—grew louder, until they were right overhead, raining machine-gun fire and bombs on us. It couldn't have gotten much worse—until it did. The tanks swayed under the force of the explosions, the bombs falling in

Unterscharführer Stettner, wearing a number of decorations.

Wilhelm Flohr, here as an Untersturmführer, commanding 5th Company.

increasing numbers. Some tanks had already been hit and were on fire. The infantry also suffered losses. The attack seemed to be ill-fated. The Russians knew that they had us trapped in a minefield, and were taking full advantage of the situation. Finally, the Pathfinders arrived and set to work, and we were soon able to resume the advance. There were still a few mines here and there; we could see the piles of earth where they'd been hastily buried. The infantry was advancing very slowly, with Russian artillery fire pinning them down. We zigzagged to avoid the mines while supporting the infantry. We finally reached the first enemy trenches and machine-gun nests, which we thought we destroyed, but they were resilient, reforming after we had passed to attack us from behind. Again, we had to halt our attack in order to clear them.

Slowly, dusk began to fall. We were smack bang in the middle of the Russian positions and we still had an enormous amount to do. The Russians, who had let us pass, were now fighting us with grenades, Molotov cocktails and anything else they could get their hands on. We had to get rid of them, and one by one, we did. Several tanks were set alight and the crews had to climb out and fight hand-to-hand with the Russians surrounding them.

Our company commander had been summoned by the regimental commander and had still not returned, leaving us disoriented. Night fell, and visibility worsened. It was quite uncomfortable. To our right, two tanks were burning. Shadows in long coats flitted around the wrecks, just visible in the flames. A few bursts from our machine guns dispersed them.

Sad news—our company commander has been killed. As he was returning from his meeting with the regimental commander, his tank was hit and exploded. It was one of the burning wrecks to our right.

Because our infantry was struggling to keep up and move forward, due to constant hand-to-hand fighting, and because we were being harassed by isolated groups of enemy fighters, our new company commander gave the order to retreat.

So, we once again had to cross the minefield, which still had many unexploded mines scattered across it. The poor light didn't help, and we had to try to follow the tracks we'd left during our advance. We were the third tank in the column. Time dragged. Sheaves of light from Russian tracers lit our way. Our engine was giving everything it had when, suddenly, we heard a deafening explosion as the tank shuddered violently and stopped. Shrapnel smacked against the sides of the vehicle, our driver swore and we knew something was badly wrong.

We had, of course, hit a mine. The tracks had broken and the suspension was badly damaged. We were in the middle of no-man's land. Fan-bloody-tastic. We got out of the tank and removed the broken track, which we laid over the back of the panzer. One of the other tanks towed us back to the lines. As we returned, we saw the driver of the company commander's tank, his face and arms badly burned, his skin peeling off in large chunks. With another tank, I made my way to the workshop to find some mechanics to fix our tank. We changed the track under a deluge of artillery fire, shrapnel whizzing past us every which way, before dismantling the damaged suspension so we could take it back to the shop to be repaired.

Over the next few days, we cleaned up the last pockets of resistance that had been holding out. The enemy bridgehead was finally eliminated. We were hit hard by the Russian artillery that had spotted us, though. A while later, the Russians evacuated their positions to retreat back across the river to the opposite bank. In the early afternoon, after clearing the terrain, we took a road to some trees behind us where we sheltered. We spent several days there as what

A young Sturmmann from the 3rd SS Panzer Regiment Totenkopf wearing the Panzer Badge.

had been assumed would be a ten-hour fight had turned into a four-day onslaught with significant losses in armor and personnel. Then again, the Russians got it just as bad.

In the valleys and gullies that had been heavily bombed by the Luftwaffe, we found the bodies of hundreds of Russians, mostly Asians, who, in the heat, already stank of decay. Aside from the soldiers, we also found dead horses, gasmasks, and fragments of uniform strewn around. At night, the foul smell of putrefying flesh drifted across to our camp, waking us up. Finally, after three days, we were relieved, having repulsed another Soviet attack that was supported by several tanks.

We moved out at midnight, returning to the village where we had left our Panzer IIIs, only to learn that our trip through the countryside would now be rerouted to Kharkov, where the Russians were trying to retake the town. We were speechless.

We swapped the Panzer IV—which had brought us nothing but bad luck—for our old Panzer III, and over the next couple of days—August 6 and 7—made our way to the station to join the convoys. Next stop: Kharkov.

Unterscharführer Stettner recalled that Friday, July 30 was hot and sunny.

Our offensive further intensified; our first objective was Hill 23.7, then 213.9, and then 174.4. From these hills, II SS Panzer Corps would surround and defeat the enemy near Marinowka. Unfortunately for us, the enemy had created large antitank barrages. It was 0800 when Hauptsturmführer Richter's heavy Tigers left the cover of a forest for a hillock north of our camp. The 1st Battalion, 3rd SS Panzer Regiment crossed no-man's land to reach the enemy lines. It was a simple task; the few remaining Russians were holed up in their trenches and would be taken care of by the following infantry.

Adolf Suwe as a Sturmmann and *Richtschutze* (gunner), wearing fashionable sunglasses.

In Profile:
Unterscharführer Kurt Arp
June 29, 1923–2010

Unterscharführer Kurt Arp in his black uniform, Totenkopf armband and Bronze Panzer Badge.

Unterscharführer Kurt Arp.

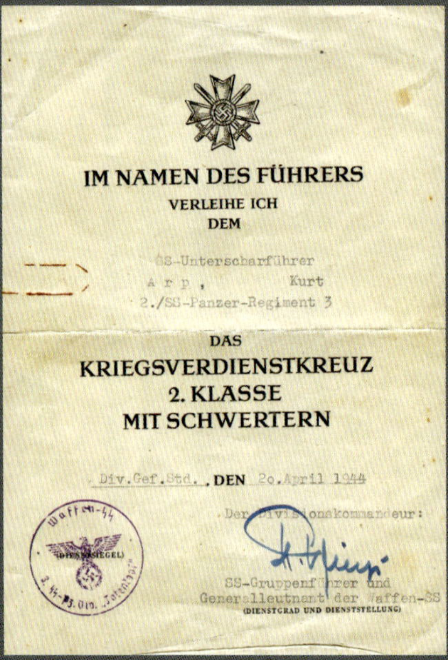

IM NAMEN DES FÜHRERS
VERLEIHE ICH
DEM

SS-Unterscharführer
Arp, Kurt
2./SS-Panzer-Regiment 3

DAS
KRIEGSVERDIENSTKREUZ
2. KLASSE
MIT SCHWERTERN

Div.Gef.Std., DEN 20.April 1944

Der Divisionskommandeur:

SS-Gruppenführer und
Generalleutnant der Waffen-SS
(DIENSTGRAD UND DIENSTSTELLUNG)

Certificate accompanying the KVK 2nd Class medal awarded to Kurt Arp.

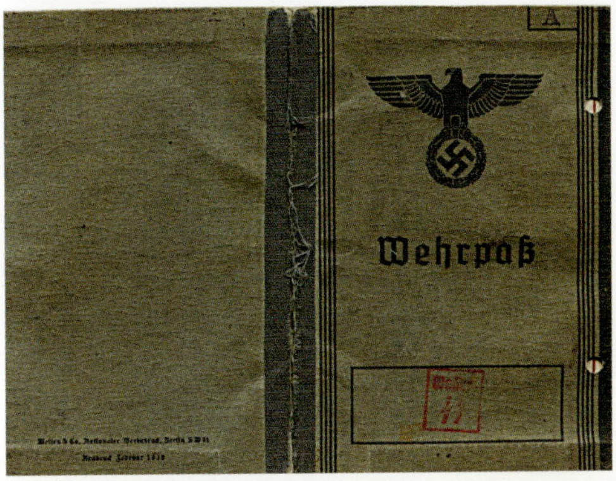

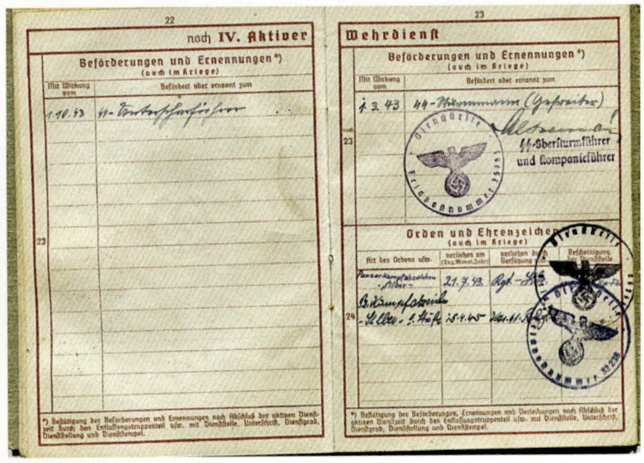

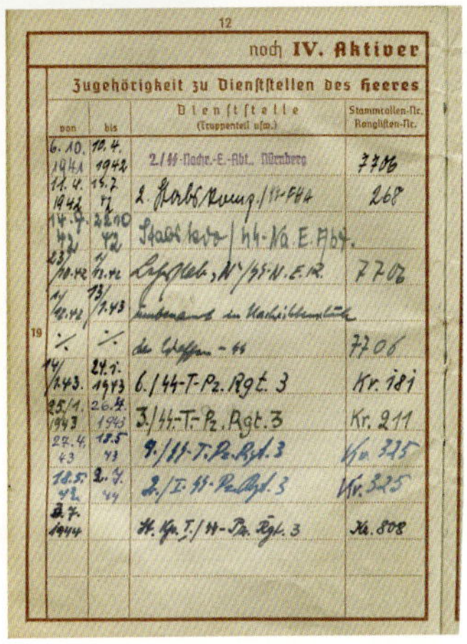

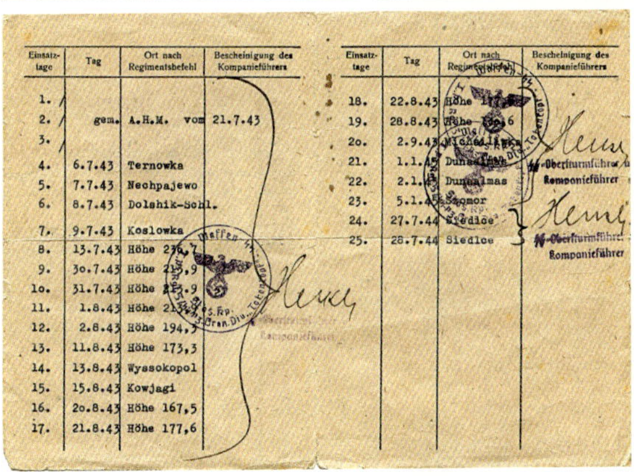

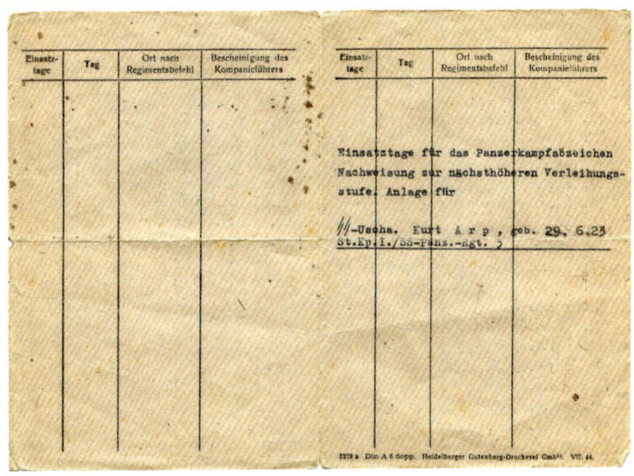

Kurt Arp's original *Wehrpass*, his paybook. The first page indicates that he was initially assigned to the signals school at Nuremburg, while another lists his later assignments, all of which were with the 3rd SS Panzer Regiment Totenkopf. His awards of the Panzer Badge in Bronze, 1st and 2nd class, are also noted, and a list of battles that Arp participated in.

Signals troops receiving awards.

In a lull during fighting, the crew of this tank set about cleaning their battle-weary vehicle and weapons. Note the machine gunner on the ground: his gun has to be kept in perfect condition to prevent problems during combat. Standing in front of the tank in his shirtsleeves is Obersturmführer Lummitsch.

Suddenly, shells rained down on the infantry and among our Panzer IVs and Tigers. Of course, it had all been too easy, and now we were approaching an antitank roadblock, the Soviet *panzerbüchsen* [antitank rifles] were nipping at our ankles. Unterscharführer Horsten's tank from 1st Company was hit, and burned with all the crew still inside. We destroyed all the antitank guns we could identify as quickly as possible, but there were so many of them. Several T-34s then appeared, but we put them out of action almost immediately. Commander Richter's tank hit a mine and was immobilized; Untersturmführer Schussler's was hit too. He lost an eye, and died in hospital sometime later from another injury. It wasn't until several more tanks were immobilized that we realized, with horror, that we were in the middle of a minefield. We called the pathfinders to help us get out, but by that time only four Tigers were still operational. Russian infantrymen and nests of machine guns and antitank guns were dealt with by artillery. The Russian lines were littered with enemy bodies including several political commissars, recognizable from their caps and blue trousers.

We came upon a new defensive line, which the Russians fought to the death to hold. To the south and northwest of Hill 213.9, were several antitank guns that the Das Reich Division had not yet reached, and these opened fired. Our Panzer IIIs and IVs suffered under their 76.2-mm fire. Untersturmführer Hostmann was shot down, as was Untersturmführer Ofner. Tanks that were damaged or had lost crewmembers retreated to regroup and replace their losses. Our tank advanced under a storm of projectiles, until an orange-blue glow appeared through the driver's periscope. The engine was silent. A cloud of black smoke gathered in the compartment but, thank God, no one was hurt. The tank gun and machine guns were still operational, but the turret couldn't turn. The gunner informed me that two neighboring tanks had hit mines. At that moment, Russian infantry attacked. We spotted them setting up mortars on a rise, but five well-placed shells put an end to them. The tanks to our left had also braked and stopped in their tracks. Our coaxial machine gun was silent, its firing pin broken. In front of us, a brave Russian soldier ran at us with a hollow charge; the radio operator's machine gun couldn't hit him … 100 meters, 80 meters, 50 meters … we fired an explosive shell that landed at his feet and killed him instantly. But there were more coming. The Russian artillery was having a grand old time, and ours was unable to retaliate as it didn't have the necessary coordinates to adjust aim without hitting our own troops in the process. Still, a battery of Nebelwerfer rocket launchers came to relieve us as best they could.

Around 1300, a squadron of Stukas appeared overhead, to destroy the Russian tanks and antitank guns. In the meantime, the pathfinders cleared two paths through the minefield.

We resumed our advance with the infantrymen hanging on to the tanks' superstructures. Shells were already falling around us, and after just 300 meters we had to halt. Hauptsturmführer Flohr ordered the infantry to get down and clear the terrain ahead. We tankers settled in for a while, then progressed to Hill 213.9. Just after we passed a depression, I saw one of our tanks hit a mine. The crew got out, uninjured, and retreated. Then we spotted a Russian 76.2-mm antitank gun 400 meters ahead of us. It fired at the tank next to us but missed. Thankfully, my gunner was a much better shot and destroyed the gun with a single round. To our left, another Panzer IV had been hit and was on fire. I swerved left, but then another tank hit a mine. Unbelievable—we were in a minefield, again! I think the Russians must have covered the entire front with them. So, we found ourselves

An excellent shot of several Panzer IIIs from the 3rd SS Panzer Regiment Totenkopf.

A Panzer IV, with *schürzen*, opens fire from the edge of a forest.

stranded and waiting for the pathfinders again. Among the tanks that had been hit was that of Hauptscharführer Schneider, commander of the 7th Company. His crew were all wounded by Russian small-arms fire, but they were all saved, except for Herbert Loth, who went missing. We covered the brave pathfinders with our fire while they were demining the area under fraught conditions. Any cap or helmet that appeared was immediately targeted by our machine guns. We couldn't take a break to urinate or eat or rest, or the Russians would fire back with a fierce intensity. We ended up using empty shell cases to relieve ourselves in—all part of being a tanker. As we passed the pathfinders, we saw the trenches where a number of Russians had died at their posts—a far cry from the Russian soldiers of 1941. I steered to the left as, on my right, three of our tanks were hit, including Hauptsturmführer Flohr's. Some of the crew were able to escape, but they were badly burned. The driver, who managed to escape, shouted that his commander was still inside, burning.

At 1625, thanks to the intervention of Paul Hausser, a group of Stukas arrived, enabling us to gain more ground and get closer to Hill 213.9. Unfortunately, Untersturmführer Moosbrucker was killed, and Untersturmführer Quarenski was seriously wounded in the process. Our losses were significant, and we were demoralized by just how many men and vehicles we were losing for each small gain. Three-quarters of the 3rd SS Panzer Regiment was out of action; 48 armored vehicles, including seven Tigers, were hit. The smoking wrecks littered the ground. Untersturmführer Tietz took over command of 5th Company.

Now that we had reached Hill 213.9, we had to get to the top of it. Progress was slow, and we had to fight for every meter by destroying the Russian infantry lines with hand grenades, hunting them down through corn fields with infantry support. I was at the head of a formation when there was a massive noise at the front of the tank—we'd been hit by a 76.2-mm antitank round. We evacuated as

> the compartment burst into flames. I was burned in several places. The loader and the gunner were already running behind me—my comrades told me that the driver and radio operator had been killed instantly. We followed our tank tracks back to the rear, where we came across a group of Russian infantry that had been overtaken by our tanks but not yet reached by our infantry. They opened fire on us. For my part, I had my MP 40 and two grenades, but my comrades only had their pistols, so I told them to hide. I crept toward the Russian machine-gunners, and rolled a grenade at them, which did the job. Then I saw one of the Russians shooting at my comrades with his PPSh-4. I fired a burst at him with my MP 40 and that took care of him. I quickly joined my men, only to find that the loader had taken a bullet to the head, and the gunner had been shot in the thigh. All further attempts to reach the top of the hill failed, with losses on both sides. We were forced to stay in our positions, within range of Russian grenades.

On August 1, 1943, the rest of 1st Battalion, under the command of Obersturmführer Gramms, and the 2nd Battalion, under Obersturmführer Walter Mattern, resumed the assault on Hill 213.9 at 1450:

> The Panzer II reserves were on standby at the rear. I took command of Flohr's tank, whose crew was a strange mix of tankers from various backgrounds. The gunner was Viennese, and previously the driver for the divisional doctor. The 1st Platoon was under the command of Unterscharführer Fischer.
>
> After an attack by the Stukas and a preparatory artillery bombardment, we attacked with the few tanks we had left. On the enemy side, anything with a barrel dispatched volleys of projectiles, but their shells fell short. It was hell, but we went through it, and despite our fear we began to advance. Tietz's tank caught fire after

A Panzer III easily mounts an incline. Note the gun glacis and additional armor.

In Profile:
Panzer IV

The Panzer IV was the panzer divisions' medium tank. The powerful 7.5-cm gun was also used by antitank teams. Note the attached antitank gun protection around the turret. This panzer is painted in a standard gray as were most new German tanks. We can see that it is a brand-new tank as there is no trace of wear and tear, or combat damage. The Panzer IV was the most widely used medium tank in the Wehrmacht, only making way for the Panzer V "Panther" later in the war.

A pair of 3rd SS Panzer Regiment long-barreled Panzer IVs, seen here mounting a rise across the steppes of the Ukraine.

A fine shot of a Panzer IV traveling at speed. Interestingly, it does not have the added protection of *schurzen* or pieces of track.

Extremely well-camouflaged Panzer IVs from the 3rd SS Panzer Regiment Totenkopf on the move across the steppe.

being hit by a well-placed shot. A motorcycle messenger arrived and told us to swing to the right. At this point, the head of our force was 300–400 meters ahead of us. To our right was Oberscharführer Sepp Fischer's tank and to our left, Uzelino's. Following behind us were the pathfinders. We were on the left flank. We had just reached a rise when Russian antitank guns opened fire. Uzelino's tank caught fire; he fell out of the turret, beside the tank, while the other crewmembers dashed to hide behind it. Shells rained on us. One of them ricocheted off my turret, and Fischer's tank was hit too. I tried to reach him by radio, but no answer—he must have been hit. I had to keep going, though the Russians were so well hidden that I couldn't see their guns. We were caught like deer in the headlights, unable to react. A shell landed right in front of my tank, throwing shrapnel and dirt over the turret. I managed to maneuver the tank into some cover behind a slight rise. It looked like ours was the last panzer left. Then Fischer's loader appeared behind me, and said: "Unterscharführer! Oberscharführer Fischer is lying beside the tank. He is badly wounded in his legs. Do you have any smoke cannisters? We want to bring the tank back to the rear to rescue the Oberscharführer. Will you cover us?" I immediately handed over some smoke cannisters, and brought the tank round to the right so I could sweep the area with fire.

To our right was the last Tiger. Suddenly, behind the carcass of a T-34, three more Russian tanks appeared on the horizon. Turret at 11 o'clock, distance 400 meters, 39 antitank shells, I had just finished my preparations when the gunner signaled that he had them in his sights. Fire! The shell landed just under the T-34's turret, which burst opened, releasing a huge eruption of flames and smoke. Nobody emerged. We fired on the other Russian tanks, destroying them one by one, with one shell apiece. Our morale perked up, replaced with elation at seeing the Russian tanks burning in front of us.

In Profile:
Hauptsturmführer Waldemar Riefkogel

January 7, 1913–July 30, 1944

SS-Hauptsturmführer und Hauptmann der Schutzpolizei Waldemar Riefkogel was born in Sarstedt, near Hanover. He was awarded the Knight's Cross on July 11, 1943, while serving as an Obersturmführer and head of 1st Company, 3rd SS Panzer Regiment. He was killed in action at Siedlce.

Waldemar Riefkogel with an injured arm as an Untersturmführer. Note that he is wearing extra warm clothing, likely provided by the Winterhilfswerk (Winter Rescue).

Waldemar Riefkogel as an Obersturmführer, standing between his Panzer III bearing the Totenkopf death's head and an Opel Blitz truck.

Waldermar Riefkogl beside a Panzer III from the 1st Company. He is wearing white overalls over his uniform, and, during a break from fighting, is having a cup of coffee (note the thermos on the tank) and a smoke.

Untersturmführer Waldemar Riefkogel in profile. He is wearing his black tanker's uniform.

An official photograph of Waldermar Riefkogel wearing his Knight's Cross. This photo gives a clear view of the division's death's head insignia, located on his collar.

Waldemar Riefkogel (left), Knight's Cross at his throat, in a dark but not tanker-black uniform.

We then turned to fire on the massed infantry, who were shocked to see us at their lines. Suddenly, Unterscharführer Tietz appeared with his tank, grinning and asking me to take command of the rest of the company, as he'd been shot in the shoulder. During the advance, he had taken a Rottenführer from the AA3 [Aufklärungsabteilung 3, or 3rd Reconnaissance Detachment] on the back of his tank. When they arrived at a trench filled with Russians, the Rottenführer got off the tank and cleared the area with his MP, but was wounded in doing so. Untersturmführer Tietz got out of the tank to rescue him but took a bullet in his shoulder. Luckily, he was still able to climb back into the tank, but was again wounded, this time by a Stalin's organ rocket fragment, near the first-aid station.

Finally, after much exertion, we took Hill 213.9 at 1600. No sooner had we reached the top than we were attacked by over 1,000 Russian infantrymen, determined to take it back. Our machine gun was silent—a stoppage—and I radioed for immediate backup. Despite our fire, the Russians continued attacking, shouting, ignoring those shot down. They were getting closer—almost within grenade range—and I was about to retreat when nine Stukas appeared overhead. I sent up an orange flare to mark our position, and they swooped, sirens screaming, dropping bombs precisely in three successive waves. Once they'd dropped their loads, the aircraft attacked the survivors, strafing them with their machine guns. We saluted the Stukas as they wheeled to return and replenish their ammunition. They had just left when the Soviet fighter-bombers arrived. I shut my turret and said a prayer. We could already hear the explosions of bombs and bursts of machine-gun fire ... but on their own troops! We were as grateful as we were shocked—their intervention had come as an unexpected boon.

We took advantage of the distraction to resume our advance. We'd just reached the next ridge when a wave of earth, fire and steel erupted in front of us. The driver

Tank 101, which belonged to the commander of the 3rd SS Panzer Regiment Totenkopf, races into action.

Two of Gerhard Treppner's comrades, Sturmmann Albrecht (left) and Sturmmann Radke. It is clear that these Sturmmänner are already veterans, wearing medal ribbons showing that they fought during the winter of 1941/42 with the Waffen-SS.

was already reversing by the time I'd finished giving the order. Now hidden behind the ridge, we were able to breathe again. Our infantry, who had been a little behind us, were now in front and clearing the Russian trenches. I watched two of our infantrymen pulling a pair of Russians out of a foxhole by their arms. The Russians were grabbing at our men's necks, trying to pull them in. Then a grenade was thrown in as the panzergrenadiers launched themselves to the side. One explosion and the Russians were dead.

By 1625, the panzers and panzergrenadiers were on the western side of the ridge. Shortly thereafter the eastern side was in our hands and the advance continued. A new antitank barrage brought our panzers to a stop. It lasted for several hours. We thought that, with the darkness, we would be able to withdraw into cover, but as soon as we started the engine, the Russian guns opened up. But by sneaking between the burned-out tank hulks, we eventually managed to get back to the infantry. Sadly, Uzelino's panzer was among the wrecks. We brought his body onto our own tank to bury him. Once we were back with the company, I heard that Fischer had been recovered and brought back successfully. He had cut

Wilhelm Flohr commander of the 5th Company in the turret of Panzer III number 555. He was killed in action on July 30, 1943.

off what was left of one of his legs with his knife, bandaged it and waited for help! He even brought his severed leg back with him, saying “It belongs to me!”

At 2200, the Russians tried to retake Hill 213.9 with fresh assaults, attacking with a battalion’s worth of men, supported by eight T-34s. Hand-to-hand combat lasted until midnight when, finally, the Russians were pushed back to their start positions.

August 3, 1943: Even though the Russians had been repulsed to the other side of the river, the fighting on the Mius had reduced companies to just a few men. NCOs were in positions of command, while battalions were barely the size of companies. The 3rd SS Panzer Regiment had just three Panzer VI Tigers, ten long-barreled Panzer IVs, one short-barreled Panzer IV, three Panzer IIIs and six armored command cars in operation.

The next day the Russian 6th Tank Army attacked with 60 T-34s. They breached our first line of defense but were stopped at the second by Sturmgeschütz and PaK guns.

On August 7, the Russians launched a massive counteroffensive and recaptured Bogoduchoff, northeast of Kharkov. They crossed the Smerla and continued attacking southwest. The panzer regiment was then transported by rail toward Kharkov. Our 5th Company was now commanded by Hauptsturmführer Nerpel. We were, with our eight Panzer IIIs, the most complete company in the battalion!

On August 10, during the night, a Russian armored attack took place to the west of Alexandrowka, supported by infantry. They ran into the 1st Battalion in the region of Walki. During the battle, the Russians were pushed back to Kowjagi, but the commander of our armored group, Obersturmführer Burgschulte, was killed. He had just poked his head out of the turret when a Russian shell struck, and he was fatally wounded.

While the 1st Battalion was fighting at Kowjagi, our 5th Company arrived at the scene to support them. We were ourselves accompanied by Schwimmwagen amphibious vehicles of the AA [Aufklärungsabteilung] which, with their MG 42 fire, swept the fields of corn and sunflowers for Russians. The enemy fled—at least, the survivors of the MG 42s did.

The Panzer Regiment had suffered heavy losses during the fighting on the Mius, and no longer had enough men to make up a full company. The 1st and 2nd Companies were merged into a single combat group, and the others into a second tactical group. By chance, Obersturmführer Riefkogel returned from convalescence following his injury, and took command of the first combat group. Supplies arrived, which increased morale. Soon enough, a new order arrived, to clear the Kowjagi sector and "take care" of any Russians who were still in the area.

There were four tanks, with Riefkogel in the lead, then Nitschke, then Steiger, and finally Baumeister. We came up against an antitank barrage. Oberscharführer Nitschke's tank was destroyed and caught fire before we were able to target the five Russian guns and eliminate them. We returned to Kowjagi, but a little while later several T-34s attacked a supply column, so Obersturmführer Riefkogel went to the rescue, destroying three of the Russian tanks and causing the others to flee.

Two hours later, Obersturmführer Riefkogel was wounded ... for the seventh time! A Russian fighter aircraft targeted his tank and shot him in the head. The commander of the regiment, Sturmbannführer Bochmann, as well as the commander of the battalion, Erwin Meierdress, were present when the crew returned with their commander. He was immediately transported to the field hospital. We were once again left without a commander for our armored group. So, the two tank groups were merged together into one, with Obersturmführer Herbatscheck, a Viennese officer, at its head.

August 1943 on the Mius Front, Panzer III 502 safely in cover in southern Ukraine. From left: gunner Werner Söldner, driver Heinz Jochum, and radio operator Reiser.

On August 15, 1943, we attacked Scharowka. On the west flank of the attack was the Deutschland Regiment, to its left was the 2nd Battalion. On our right, Russian fire. The corn field was soon cleared and we arrived at Sotnaja village. As we were passing through, the villagers told us that, a little earlier, the Russians had fled with 12 tanks. We positioned ourselves at the exit of the village and swept the fields with our fire for any Russian infantrymen still lurking. Now on our right were other tanks from our battalion. We turned northeast and, over a wide front, passed through a small valley. A group of Russian tanks appeared around 2,000 meters ahead of us—first 30, then 40 of them—and were soon directly in front of us. We saw them cross a field of sunflowers, crushing the flowers under their tracks. Apparently, they hadn't spotted us yet, and turned to the left toward a hedgerow. In our headsets, we could hear Commander Bochmann giving orders to the Tigers and Panzers to open fire. Distance: 1,600 meters. The right flank of the enemy group was entrusted to us Panzer IIIs. Already, we could see the plumes from T-34s that had been hit. The valley reverberated with gunfire. We got into position and opened fire, but at a lesser distance than our comrades. We stopped counting how many Russian tanks we hit as we were now being targeted by antitank fire. The 2nd Battalion withdrew; we would collect our damaged tanks later.

I was then wounded during a clash with a Russian antitank gun, and was brought back to Kowjagi. All along the road were fresh graves. The 1st Battalion Speiss had laid a Hagal Rune [a cross specific to the Waffen-SS] on a mound where some comrades from the 3rd SS Panzer Regiment Totenkopf had been laid to rest. I read the names on the cross: Ostuf. Burgschulte, Ostuf. Altermiller, Hscha. Seifert. I couldn't believe my eyes. We had all been together not long ago—Rudi Seifert and I had even served in the same tank.

Werner Söldner wrote on the back of this photo at Merefa, Ukraine, in August 1943: "It wasn't always this quiet!"

Kharkov to the Dnieper

At Kharkov, the Totenkopf was assigned, along with the 2nd SS Panzer Division Das Reich, to stymie Operation *Rumyantsev*, the Soviet offensive designed to capture the city, in what became known as the fourth battle of Kharkov. With their flanks threatened, the Waffen-SS was forced to abandon the city, on August 23, 1943. The Soviet juggernaut was increasingly unstoppable as the Wehrmacht was relentlessly squeezed westward, back across the Dnieper. At the town of Krivoi Rog, on the Ukrainian–Romanian border, the Totenkopf was to fight its last battle on Soviet soil.

Kharkov was now barely recognizable, as Weber recalled: "Trains full of refugees were steaming out toward the west. Artillery thundered through the skies, which were full of Stukas flying over the city on their way to drop bombs in the near vicinity. Bridges were being prepared for demolition."

> After a few hours, we had replenished our supplies of fuel, ammunition, and rations, and were ready for battle. Which was just as well, as the Russians were trying to surround us. Eight kilometers were still open, so we had to get out of there during the night. That evening, we left via the heaving roads, soldiers and refugees alike leaving the coming battlefield.
>
> The next day, the platoons were assigned to other units. Ours was to support the reconnaissance unit of the SS Totenkopf Division, which was engaged in

On the neverending steppes, Panzer IIIs with *schürzen* head for the front with a squadron of Stukas flying overhead.

A Panzer III from 2nd Company passes through a Soviet village. Note the fuel drum on the back.

> ferocious combat with the Russians. We set off without delay to reach our new position alongside the SS-AA3 before nightfall.
>
> We halted just before arriving, as our platoon leader had gone ahead to scout for the reconnaissance group's command post. He returned with the news that there was a large force of enemy tanks with supporting infantry preparing to attack. We had to prepare ourselves for battle.
>
> The front in this sector was peculiar: on the outskirts of a village, in the middle of a forest, was a *kolkhoz* [a collective farm] which in fact comprised just two buildings separated by a narrow forest road.

The Totenkopf reconnaissance group's command post was set up inside one of those buildings; the other, apparently, was home to the Soviet HQ. This bizarre situation was further complicated by the fact that at night the village was under Russian control, and during the day under German.

> When we entered with our tanks, along the path between the two buildings, we opened fire with our tank guns and machine guns against the Russian-held *kolkhoz*, setting fire to the building before continuing on our way. One day, the Russians left an old T-34 behind a shed. We thought it was abandoned, but as our column passed, it opened fire on us three or four times. After that day, we were a lot more suspicious of apparent wrecks left out by the Russians.
>
> Now and again, we supported localized counterattacks, and it was during one of these that our company commander was accidently killed. We were being attacked by a Russian tank, and the whole platoon had opened fire on it. Unfortunately, one of our shells hit the company commander's tank. He was killed alongside two members of his crew. The same evening, the Russians attacked with a large number of tanks, which forced us to draw back until we encountered a Sturmgeschütz unit, which helped us to stop the enemy.
>
> But soon, the Russians renewed their attack, launching multiple assaults. We had no respite and were fighting on all fronts at once, our attention turned to

wherever was burning the fiercest. It seemed we were in constant demand. Our armored group was the reconnaissance group's sweetheart: they were always calling for us, demanding our attention, asking us for things.

The Russians did not pose too much of a threat to us at that time, as they only had a few heavy tanks. But with their incessant attacks, the front was constantly changing. We went back and forth and left and right, and one day found ourselves incorporated into a company of infantry. Our armored group was reduced at that time to six tanks, but morale was still high as, despite the fact we had been surrounded alongside the infantrymen, we knew that other units from the division were on their way.

The next day, we were camouflaged in a wheat field when we spotted a group of tanks in the distance. They could only be ours, we thought, coming to our rescue. They were so far away that we couldn't even see them distinctly with our binoculars. Calmly, they approached, until Luftwaffe fighter-bombers strafed them, blowing up three and sending the rest fleeing. We were horrified at the aviators' mistake, as we were convinced they were German tanks. But soon the truth dawned on us, and we too opened fire on the retreating—Russian—tanks.

The Soviet assaults continued, as they were keen to close the pocket they'd trapped us in, which was now no more than 600 or 700 meters in diameter. The enemy brought in many more armored vehicles and antitank guns: they were clearly preparing for a big attack. We positioned two armored vehicles at the entrance to the village and set fire to the buildings. We had infantry everywhere in and around the village. Bursts of fire from machine guns and rifles were heard that night. But the attack did not come.

The next morning, we went out on a recce with three armored vehicles, in the direction of the German-controlled railway station. We came across two Russian

A battle-weary Oberscharführer Ratzayzak, Kharkov, 1943.

In Profile:
Sturmmann Leopold Jahrstorfer

May 13, 1924–April 27, 1996

Leopold Jahrstorfer in his black uniform and helmet.

Sturmmann Leopold Jahrstorfer, with Panzer Badge.

Besitzzeugnis

Dem SS - Rottenführer

Leopold Jahrstorfer

8./SS-Panzer-Regiment 3

verleihe ich für tapfere Teilnahme an 26 Einsatztagen die II. Stufe zum

Panzerkampfabzeichen in Silber

Rgt.Gef.Std., den 16.1.45.

SS-Sturmbannführer
u.Rgt.-Kommandeur.

A certificate accompanying the Panzer Badge, 2nd class in Silver for 26 days in combat awarded to Leopold Jahrstorfer, 8th Company, 3rd SS Panzer Regiment Totenkopf.

Sturmmann Leopold Jahrstorfer on a civilian motorcycle.

During the fighting at Kharkov, two combat-tested Totenkopf officers carefully survey the front lines.

armored vehicles as a railwayman signaled a train in and let the men board without raising the alarm! Shortly before arriving at the station, we were shot at from a corn field. We stopped and retaliated against these invisible enemies, before heading into the field to hunt down the survivors.

In the corn field while searching for the recalcitrant Russians, we spotted a possible escape route as, it appeared, we were not completely surrounded after all. There was a chance that, by taking a narrow road following the edge of a forest for 500 or 600 meters, we could actually escape the cauldron. There were Soviet antitank guns positioned at the edge the forest, so, in single file, we stormed the positions and opened fire. I destroyed three guns myself. One of them returned fire, but most of the teams chose to flee, so only one of our vehicles was hit. It took a hit in the engine and stopped, but was soon towed back to the command post. The infantry, who had stayed in the village, joined us the next day, bringing in more prisoners.

A few clashes developed over the next few days, but nothing serious enough to cause us any losses. Sometime later, our combat group was dissolved and we rejoined our company, where we spent several days resting before the fighting recommenced.

Finally, new orders arrived.

We prepared our tanks as usual and drove off—into the sunset, no less—toward the jump-off points for our new objective. We reached a pine forest that would hide us from view and from aerial attack. We'd be launching our assault from here the next day.

The following morning, we were woken, not only by the bright sunshine but also by shouts of "Hurrah" from a horde of attackers bearing down on us. A group of Bolsheviks was trying to attack us, but they were quickly annihilated. Around midday, we began our advance. We encountered no opposition on the road, and arrived at a *kolkhoz* where we would stay for the night.

Our new orders arrived around mid-afternoon the next day. We prepared the tank and drove to the departure point for the next offensive, which we reached at sunset. Since it was too late to do anything further that day, we hid our tanks in a pine forest for the night.

Around midday, our offensive began, but we met with no opposition. We stopped en route at a *kolkhoz* to spend the night. A group of infantrymen, supported by our tanks, resumed the attack the next morning, but we soon encountered serious resistance and we were unable to continue. A temporary withdrawal enabled us to change direction to circumvent the Russians. As night fell, we went onto the offensive, crossing a field that had also recently been harvested, with sheaves of grain assembled in piles here and there. We approached the Russian lines without being seen, thanks to the undulations of the ground, which we used to our advantage. We stopped on a small rise and, from there, rained hell down on the Russian lines. A light fog settled over the landscape, masking the depression where the Russians were positioned. Suddenly they returned fire. The sky was illuminated as if by lightning; the sheaves of grain appeared to dance in the flickering light. The Russian heavy artillery, which had so far been silent, began shelling us from a good distance away. We responded in kind. The battle lasted late into the night. We reached a sunflower field later that night, and stopped to camouflage our tanks and await the next exchange of fire.

The next day was quiet. We contacted our artillery and gave them the coordinates of a T-34 that was out of range of our 5-cm guns. It would have been a waste of our ammunition had we tried, so we let the artillery boys use it for target practice. The rest of the day passed uneventfully, and in the evening we moved. At our new position, we dug our sleeping holes under the tanks. Several days passed without incident; the heat of the sun weighed us down during the day, and at night, curled up in our holes, we shivered as the Russian artillery lulled us to sleep. Sometimes Soviet fighter aircraft flew over, dropping smoke to mark our position, or a few bombs here and there.

The summer faded, little by little, as the warm sunshine was replaced by the first of the rain and cold. We were now retreating non-stop, leaving us with little free time, but we took the opportunity to lend a hand to the men in the repair shop who were fixing up our tank and others that weren't so badly damaged. At night, the skies glowed red from the light of burning villages and fields that our infantry had laid waste to. Herds of cows and pigs formed long columns, moving west. Everyone seemed to be heading toward the new line of resistance beyond the Dnieper, which we hoped we would be able to hold for a long time. New weapons were waiting for us there, but I suspected it wouldn't be enough to turn the tide.

After passing through Poltava, Krementschug and some other towns, we finally reached the Dnieper early one morning in early autumn 1943. We crossed the great river by ferry and settled into our new positions on the far bank. We

Officers from the 3rd SS Panzer Regiment Totenkopf share a meal with their infantry comrades.

Members of the 3rd SS Panzer Regiment Totenkopf. The Sturmmann, second from left, has already been decorated, showing his experience on the front. The photo is dated December 7, 1943.

had been expecting solid trenches, bunkers, and other pre-prepared buildings, but there was nothing, just what the troops constantly flowing through the camp had built themselves. Of course, the Russians were nipping at our heels and did not allow us to establish strong positions; we couldn't stop them from crossing the river and pushing us further back, even closer to the fatherland.

We received orders to withdraw, to take up positions in reserve. This involved negotiating several minefields, and though they were well cleared and marked out by the pathfinders, it was still stressful. When we arrived at our new positions the following day, the deadly dance recommenced. Masses of T-34s attacked us, seemingly unperturbed by the minefields. They had almost reached our lines when we retaliated. Very quickly, three Russian tanks were blown up. My own company was not involved in the fight though, so we watched the tank duel from our positions. We spent the day quietly observing the action while reinforcing our defenses. The night, too, was quiet for us, as we were well camouflaged in a wheat field.

In the early hours of the morning, we changed position in preparation for a new assault against the Soviet armor. All day, we could hear the random firing of a lone Russian tank. It hadn't seen us, so we didn't know what it was shooting at. Unfortunately, our commander was then wounded; he was in his turret when a shell exploded nearby. We had to take him to the field hospital and, having no tank commander available, we went about our business without command for the rest of the day and into combat. Indeed, the Russian tanks attacked as soon as night fell, the infantry shouting "Hurrah!" We went to meet them (without our commander), escorted by our infantry, who attacked in groups. We went over a rise with our company and, completely stunned, saw the Russian infantry gathering behind our own tanks, so we about-faced and blasted them with tank and machine-gun fire. I don't think the Russians could make us out properly in the darkness. One of our tanks had plunged right into the Russian troops to save a PaK gun that had been overwhelmed, though the team was fighting tooth and nail to defend themselves. The PaK team managed to climb onto the tank and return to our lines with their wounded. The same tank was hit not long afterwards by a Soviet *Ratsch-Bumm* [76-mm divisional gun M1942 (ZiS-30)] but the crew managed to get out and rejoin us without casualties.

The Russians continued attacking throughout the early hours, but failed to penetrate our lines. When the sun came up, we changed positions and took our turn on the offensive. The barrage from the Russian tanks and antitank guns was so intense that it almost swamped us—we had to call in the Stukas to clear the ground. Several bombs fell close to us as we advanced on the enemy positions. I'm sure the Soviets had a good laugh at us being shot at by our own aircraft. After we sent up a few white smoke signals, the pilots realized their mistake and dropped the rest of their payloads on the Russians.

Our new tank commander arrived just before the second attack began. He had lost his own tank during the first attack after it had been hit by an antitank shell. We also received reinforcements in the form of three or four infantrymen per tank, to fight the Soviet infantry who were trying to take us out with portable antitank weapons and Molotov cocktails.

This massive Soviet KV-1, knocked out and abandoned, is being inspected by members of the Totenkopf Division.

Gerhard Treppner in his black uniform, wearing his Totenkopf armband and War Merit Cross ribbon.

In Profile: Rottenführer Gerhard Treppner

February 26, 1922–September 15, 2004

Gerhard Treppner as an Unterscharführer.

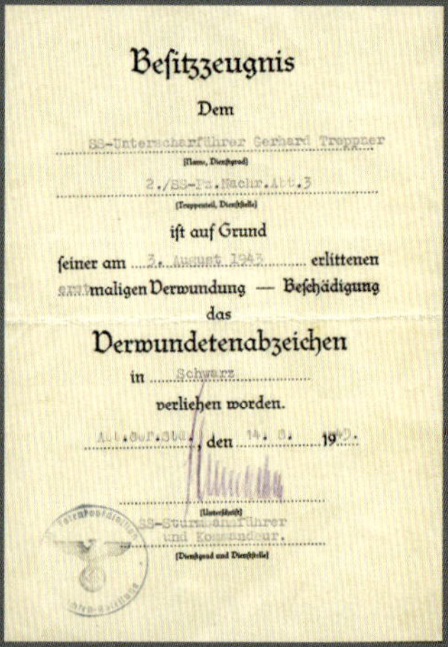

Besitzeugnis

Dem

SS-Unterscharführer Gerhard Treppner

(Name, Dienstgrad)

2./SS-Pz.Nachr.Abt.3

(Truppenteil, Dienststelle)

ist auf Grund

seiner am 2. August 1943 erlittenen

maligen Verwundung — Beschädigung

das

Verwundetenabzeichen

in Schwarz

verliehen worden.

den 1943.

(Unterschrift)

SS-Sturmbannführer und Kommandeur

(Dienstgrad und Dienststelle)

Certificate accompanying the Wound Badge awarded to Unterscharführer Treppner, 3rd SS Panzer Nachrichten Battalion Totenkopf.

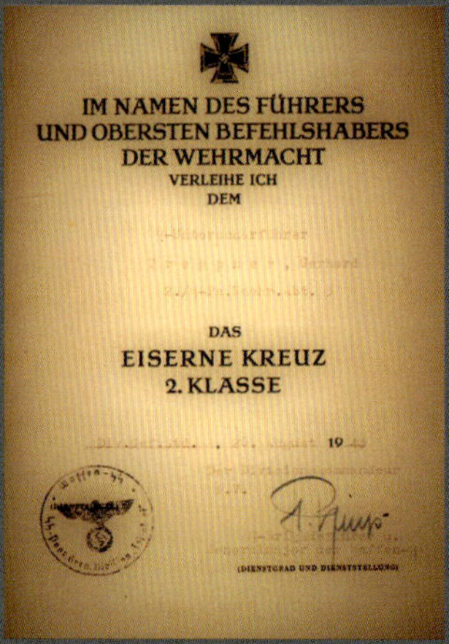

IM NAMEN DES FÜHRERS UND OBERSTEN BEFEHLSHABERS DER WEHRMACHT VERLEIHE ICH DEM

DAS EISERNE KREUZ 2. KLASSE

19

(DIENSTGRAD UND DIENSTSTELLUNG)

IM NAMEN DES FÜHRERS UND OBERSTEN BEFEHLSHABERS DER WEHRMACHT VERLEIHE ICH DEM

Treppner, Gerhard

DAS KRIEGSVERDIENSTKREUZ 2. KLASSE MIT SCHWERTERN

Div. Gef. Std., DEN 20. April 1943

(DIENSTGRAD UND DIENSTSTELLUNG)

Certificate accompanying the Iron Cross 2nd class belonging to Gerhard Treppner.

Rottenführer Gerhard Treppner behind one of the unit's vehicles.

Certificate accompanying the War Merit Cross 2nd class with swords awarded to Rottenführer Gerhard Treppner, 2nd Company, 3rd SS Panzer Nachrichten Battalion.

Draped with infantry, we drove slowly toward a corn field, which presented us with a challenge. As we approached, we could see the Russians watching us from their foxholes. Antitank rifle fire came from the left, ricocheting off our armor, so the commander decided to drive right over the antitank nests. We accelerated to crush them, as our infantry escort jumped to the ground to finish them off.

In front of us was a large mound of earth, behind which two Russians stood with their antitank rifle. We had already driven over them when two dull thuds sounded inside the tank. A thick yellow smoke rapidly invaded the tank. Someone stood on my feet—the driver, I think. I couldn't see a thing. The tank continued to move forward. I opened my trapdoor to try to see what was going on outside. The commander, despite the danger, also stuck his head outside the tank into the pungent yellow smoke to try and guide the driver to reverse away, so we could assess the damage. He gave orders to the driver to this effect. Only the radio operator stayed silent, and for good reason: he had put his gasmask on.

We managed to pull back enough to check the tank over. As we were exiting the infantry looked at us wide-eyed as if they had seen a ghost. From what they told us, it seemed no one had thought our panzer crew would make it out alive. A bright, intense fire had apparently enveloped the tank, and, upon further examination, we could see why: some Russian infantrymen had thrown bottles full of phosphorus at us, and they'd landed right by the air filters. It was through sheer luck that they hadn't set fire to the engine. Instead, the toxic phosphorus gas had filled the tank compartment.

After airing out the tank, we got back in and rejoined the company, which had advanced significantly. We drove to a low rise, at the top of which we found ourselves face to face with a 47-mm Russian antitank gun. We didn't have any explosive shells left, so instead we fired two antitank shells

An Unterscharführer tank commander from the 3rd SS Panzer Regiment Totenkopf in the turret of his panzer, with his headset.

Werner Söldner, 3rd SS Panzer Regiment, who supplied many of the photos in this book.

that destroyed the shield and the sight respectively, removing any threat it might have posed. We swung round to the right and, once again, found ourselves in front of another 47-mm gun. Clearly it had been waiting for us, and fired a shell at the turret in welcome. We reciprocated with our antitank shells, but I don't think we hit it at all. After receiving three more hits to the turret, there was another flash of light, this time from a Russian tank, which destroyed our gun.

It was time to get out of this nest of vipers. We set the turret to 10 o'clock in the hope that the enemy wouldn't see that the gun was damaged, and retreated just beyond range of the Russian guns. Then we made our way to a village where we found a repair shop.

The next day, under Soviet artillery fire, we moved out and withdrew farther back, in order to continue our repairs. We stayed there for several weeks as the replacement parts, notably a new barrel for the gun, were not immediately available. We took no part in any further action after that.

Heinz Fickert served on general staff of the 3rd SS Panzer Regiment, which, at the end of October 1943, was to be found in a small village in the Ukraine.

An Unterscharführer received the order from the commander, Sturmbannführer Bochmann, to reconnoiter the terrain where our next tank battle would take place. He asked a driver to accompany him in a Schwimmwagen, which was what happened. Arriving at a ridge, the Unterscharführer ordered his comrade in the Schwimmwagen to conceal himself, while he climbed the ridge. Through his binoculars he was able to observe the upcoming battlefield. He then heard the sound of Russian machine-gun fire, some 500 meters away. It was answered by a flurry of MG 42 fire, nicknamed "Hitler's saw" due to its 1,200 rounds-per-minute cadence. Our infantry must have been tackling the Russians behind the hillock.

Meanwhile, the driver was sitting in his Schwimmwagen, waiting for the Unterscharführer to return. Suddenly, an infantryman appeared at the car and asked the driver to take a seriously wounded man back to camp. The driver, of course, had his orders to wait for the NCO, but the soldier was shouting that it was an emergency, that his friend was losing a lot of blood. After a moment's hesitation, the driver decided to rescue the wounded man.

A large, flat expanse was visible from the top of the hill, and around 200 meters out was one of our MG 42 nests. The gunner had been badly wounded in the thigh, and was indeed bleeding heavily. The Russians were close. The driver and the infantryman quickly lifted the injured man into the back seat of the car and bandaged his wound as best they could to stem the flow of blood before speeding away. The whole rescue lasted only a few minutes. The driver followed the signposts to the field hospital, passing an ambulance that had been attacked by some unscrupulous partisans. After dropping off their wounded comrade, the two men returned to their positions, just two kilometers back along the road.

Back at the ridge, the Unterscharführer was waiting. As the infantryman returned to his position, the NCO scolded the driver for disobeying orders. When they arrived back at the HQ, he also ordered the driver to scrub the back seat, which was bloody from the rescue. I still wonder if that wounded man survived the war. I hope he did. And Unterscharführer, if you're still alive, I'm sorry for keeping you waiting on that ridge.

Fritz Edelman remembers his days serving as a Rottenführer in the 2nd Battalion, 3rd SS Panzer Regiment Totenkopf in Russia in late 1943/early 1944:

A Panzer IV in a forest. It has been painted white and has *schürzen* on its sides and turret.

Unterscharführer Alwin Rung (left) with a comrade from the 6th Company. He has been decorated with the Panzer Badge in Silver, the Wound Badge and the Iron Cross 2nd class.

At the beginning of December 1943, the combat group of the 3rd SS Panzer Regiment (2nd Battalion and the regiment's Heavy Company) was located at Nowo Petrowka. Alongside two other crews, we had set up our quarters in a Russian *izba* [farmhouse]. On January 6, 1944, we were given a warning order. We had to link up with the Heer's 13th Panzer Division at Ingulo-Kamenka. This we achieved during the night, during heavy snow flurries. In the morning fog, the attack began. Suddenly, we heard shots coming from the right. A panzer from the 7th Company had taken a direct hit and could not move. We fired at a haystack just to our right, and sure enough there was a T-34 hiding behind it, which retreated as soon as it saw us. We had stumbled upon an antitank barrage. We regrouped and got into new positions, as the fog had now dissipated. As we were at the head of the formation, we were the first to reach the top of a small rise, from which we saw a massive column of trucks and sleds on the march.

The commander, Oberscharführer Horst Marx, said to the driver, "Artur, forward!", then a few seconds later, "Enemy positions—fire at will!" Through our headsets, we heard the commander instructing other tanks to fire on the Russian column. Our 5-cm KwK gun and machine guns threw everything we had at the moving targets 500 meters ahead of us. Soon, we heard the voice of Haupsturmführer Neidhardt: "Marx, antitank guns at 2 o'clock!" We continued our advance, stopping to fire on a KV-1 tank that our gunner, Erich Jurgeit, had targeted.

Everything seemed to be happening so quickly. I fired on the column with my machine gun, but then we were fired on, and our engine was hit. The tank went up in flames. The order to evacuate didn't reach me, as all the communications were destroyed in the explosion. Luckily, I still had my wits about me, and when I found the turret turned and blocking my exit, I made for the loader's door, which was open. I had to go through the flames licking over the engine compartment and jump to the ground, where the crew were waiting for me. I was dismayed to find that Erich Jurgeit had been killed in the explosion.

We were still being targeted by enemy fire, so we had to run to get back to our own lines, carrying the body of our friend. The next day, we found quarters with another crew, and kept watch in conditions of -35 degrees. We managed to recover our tank, but it was badly damaged, so we took it to Dolinskaja, where we found a repair shop. This was also where we buried our friend Erich.

After that, SS-Rottenführer Peter Kampf received Panzer III number 524 from the same repair shop—the driver was Rottenführer Schiel, the gunner was Sturmmann Hermann Fath, and the loader was Hubert Colin. I was brought on board as the radio operator. On our way to Kirovgrad, driving through the night, we arrived at the front, ready for a fresh attack on Bolschaja Wiska. The 2nd Battalion combat group was under the orders of Hauptsturmführer Neidhardt, and while it should have been in the second line, it ended up next to us in the front line. The advance got off to a good start, and we pushed the Russians back towards Andrejewka, where the enemy's second defensive line was situated.

It was approaching midday when the tank in front of us, commanded by Untersturmführer Jurda, hit a mine and was immobilized. The crew evacuated the tank and, armed with handguns, pistols, and MP 40s, made a dash for our infantry, who were just behind us. We were continuing to advance when a T-34,

A panzer crew cleaning the gun barrel.

which had been lying in ambush, fired at us. A gas canister situated behind the turret caught fire. The loader got out through the turret to cut it loose and was hit by Russian machine-gun fire. The smoke from the burning gas began to invade the compartment and the engine. We fired back at the offending T-34, which in turn caught fire. Then the tank commander ordered us to evacuate. The engine was well and truly done for. We left the tank and I lost consciousness for a few seconds, before being woken up by the ammunition in our tank cooking off in the flames. We ran towards Jurda's tank, which was empty, and took cover underneath it. I was hit by a machine-gun bullet so we had to get out from under the tank to pack the wound, and while we were in the open, I felt a massive impact on my back—I had been shot again! It was a machine gun and was firing non-stop. Luckily, I was still able to move, so I stayed down and slid myself toward the body of a Russian soldier lying nearby. I grabbed the Russian's PPSh-41 submachine gun, which was fully loaded, and stayed there for a good two hours while a group of Russians from Andrejewka, approached. Our infantry had surrounded the village and chased out the Reds. We heard some guns firing and houses burning. Our howitzers and 7.5-cm infantry guns fired on the retreating troops; their projectiles were landing closer and closer to us. I saw Hermann Fath stretched out on the ground, and called out to him. No response—he was dead. After what seemed like an eternity, I heard a small group of four or five Russians busying themselves around Jurda's tank. I pulled myself up to my knees and fired 3 or 4 bursts from the PPSh-41 at them. Then I fell backward, and found myself in a shell crater, where Sturmmann Reisser and Jurda's radio operator were hiding, both of them wounded. We waited for nightfall to try and get to the village, where we knew our comrades had established a firm base. We made it, somehow, and were greeted by the 6th Company, 6th SS Panzergrenadier Regiment. Their doctor gave us first aid before sending us off to the company field hospital. Hauptsturmführer Neidhardt visited us there.

Members of the 3rd SS Panzer Regiment Totenkopf in the lee of an *izba*.

A young Waffen-SS officer in his reversible winter overalls.

Unterscharführer Stettner recalled:

> It made my stomach turn to see the speed with which the Heer's troops retreated without really trying that hard to fight back. But what could we do? Orders are orders, and the Russians were thus able to retake the terrain without a fight. Finally, we were halted and the retreat ended. Our armored regiment was reassembled, with a few new tanks and some fresh troops bolstering our ranks. But we could only form one battalion. The extra the men were sent to Germany to collect new tanks and reinforcements before rejoining us at a later date.
>
> Companies were formed into battle groups—*kampfgruppen*—and sent into battle, but there was not much for our regiment to do. Slowly, winter arrived and the Russians continued their inexorable advance. We had given up our old but faithful Panzer IIIs and found ourselves alongside the transportation corps at Dolinskaja. It was all quite calm. When we heard the sound of gunfire and fighting in the distance, we started preparing our defenses in front of the village.
>
> By December 17, 1943, we had effectively become infantrymen. A thick layer of snow covered the entire landscape, and it was very cold. The Russians calmly held the neighboring town. Then, everything started to happen. We were replaced by a fresh armored division, which immediately went on the offensive, so we were able to return to the village to spend a peaceful night in bed. Even better, I was granted leave to go home, which was the best news I could have received. One of my comrades had also be granted leave, so we both caught a freight train to Odessa, then to Kowel, and finally a special train for soldiers on leave took us back to Germany. At 3 a.m. on December 27, 1943, I was, at last, home.
>
> My 21 days' leave passed in a flash. On January 18, 1944, I had to return to the front, and on January 31, I was back with my company, which had changed quite dramatically since my departure. The same day, I replaced a comrade on the front

Portrait of Sturmbannführer Georg "Schorch" Bochmann, wearing the Knight's Cross.

In Profile: Oberführer Georg Bochmann

September 18, 1913–June 8, 1973

Born in Albernair, Saxony, Georg Bochmann was awarded the Knight's Cross on May 3, 1942, as commander of the 3rd SS Panzerjager Battalion; the Oak Leaves on May 17, 1943 as commander of the 2nd Motorized Battalion of the "Thule" Regiment of the Totenkopf; and the Swords as commander of the Horst Wessel Division on March 30, 1945. He died in Offenbach, as a result of injuries sustained during the war.

Sturmbannführer "Schorch" Bochmann, this time wearing his black tanker's uniform. He commanded the 2nd Battalion, 3rd SS Panzer Regiment Totenkopf.

Georg Bochmann during a training exercise.

A rare photo taken during combat of Georg Bochmann in his shirtsleeves in the summer of 1943.

Wir wollen auch im
Gebete
gedenken unseres zweiten Sohnes, über
dessen Schicksal wir noch im
Ungewissen sind:

Johann Mitterbauer

Oberschütze im Stabe eines Panzerregiments

geboren am 4. Dezember 1923
vermißt bei den Abwehrkämpfen im
Osten, im Raume Golta-Perwomeisk,
seit 21. März 1944.

Weilt er noch unter den Lebenden, dann möge unser Gott im Trost und Stärke sein.

Hat er sein Leben aber bereits in die Hände Gottes zurückgegeben, dann möge der Herr ihm den ewigen Frieden schenken.

Death notice for Oberschütze Johann Mitterbauer from the 3rd SS Panzer Regiment Totenkopf. He was reported missing on March 21, 1944.

line and was back in the thick of things. But the front was quiet—it was good when it was quiet. We spent two days in advanced positions then returned to the village for two days. We were set up in very comfortable quarters and where we felt very at home. We stayed up playing cards until late at night, and each company spoiled its men with food. We lived very well for a while.

The battalion now had no more than eight tanks. One day, we received an order to report to the railway workshop: we were to go out and recover all the vehicles that had been bogged down or frozen by frost in undesirable places. We were not impressed that we had to leave our comfortable lodgings to go and dig vehicles out of the mud and ice.

But all good things must come to an end. One week later, we returned to the front, as we were expecting a big Soviet offensive at any time. We waited for them in well-prepared positions and in bunkers. They didn't come. Now and again we were put on alert, without knowing why or what was happening. We even decorated our bunker with trinkets and bits and pieces to make it a bit more homely. Sometimes the Russian artillery made some noise to let us know that they were still there. When it was clear that the attack wasn't going to happen, we were sent to the rear to resume our repair and rescue work. Bad weather had made the roads impassable for a lot of vehicles, and getting them unstuck was exhausting work, the mud always hindering our efforts. We were working harder than ever. Troops coming back from the front clogged up the roads, so the Russian fighter-bombers were having a field day—not that they managed to hit much.

Balta to Radzymin

By mid-April 1944, the bulk of the Totenkopf Division was encamped at Balta, in the Trifesti–Carligu–Negresti sector of Romania. The division had crossed the Bug after an attempt to relieve the German troops encircled in the Korsun Pocket, and had fought at the subsequent battle of Kirovgrad that had seen the panzer divisions forced back to the Dniester. After a period of reorganization, when the Totenkopf was equipped with new Panther tanks, the division halted a Soviet offensive at Târgu Frumos, before redeployment to Poland in early July.

Walter Weber takes up the story:

> Our regiment gathered at Nowa Ukrainka—at least, what was left of it did. The area around the railway station was full of damaged vehicles, all due to be loaded onto trains to be repatriated to Germany. It wasn't easy for us because we constantly had about 20 Russian tanks on our backs, trying to overwhelm us. Nevertheless,

A column of Totenkopf Panzer IIIs moving through a forest near Kolotajew. The additional armor and the three-bar insignia are distinctive.

> we drove them back each time, causing them losses as we went about loading the broken-down vehicles. It took us two full days, but eventually we finished the job without the Russians causing too much disruption.
>
> Our own tanks were loaded onto the last train and we left Nowo Ukrainka under fire from Russian artillery. We detrained at Balta station and, with two tanks, were tasked with defending the place.

At Balta the troops had access to stores of sugar and salt, which they could exchange with the locals for other foods, enabling them to stockpile stores. However, the Russians were putting pressure on the city:

> One morning, we were rudely awoken by the din of heavy firing. Our mascot, a dog called Hanomag, ran into our room, barking loudly. We had saved him during the fighting sometime earlier, and adopted him. We sprang out of bed and quickly dressed, learning as we did that a group of Russians had infiltrated under the cover of darkness and had managed to capture a few outlying houses. Another unit had reacted quickly, counterattacked and pushed the Russians back, without the need for us to intervene. Things calmed down and we went back to bed, but stayed alert.
>
> The same thing happened the next day, but with more intensity. This time, the Russians used high-explosive rounds and again took control of some houses. Luckily, they didn't see our panzer, or they would have destroyed it before we had a chance to get into it. With the help of a Flakvierling, we fought them off, leaving their dead scattered across the ground, before chasing them and making an even larger dent in their ranks. Even against ground targets, the Flakvierling was a formidable weapon.
>
> That evening, we positioned ourselves on the outskirts of the town. It was quiet, but we knew more attacks were coming; before long we were proved right, as artillery began pounding us. Our good times were gone. It sounded like we were

Untersturmführer Kwarinski and Oberscharführer Ratzayzak.

In Profile:

Oberschütze Adolf Albers

January 20, 1924–?

Above: Sturmmann Adolf Albers in his black tanker's uniform.

Left: A young SS-Schütze Adolf Albers, 5th Company, 3rd SS Panzer Regiment Totenkopf.

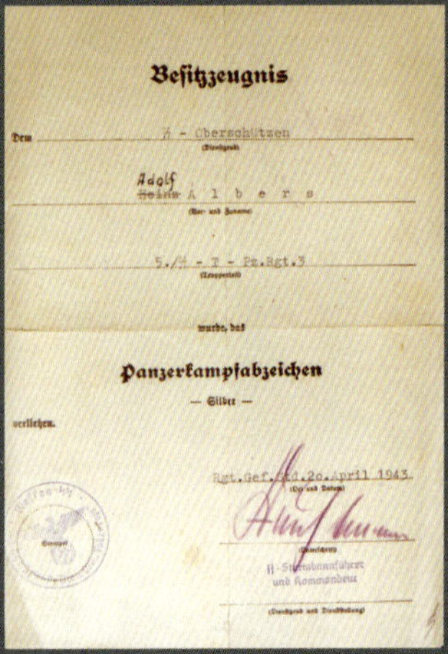

Besitzzeugnis

Dem ﾠ ﾠ ﾠ ﾠ SS - Oberschützen

Adolf Albers

5./SS - T - Pz.Rgt.3

wurde das

Panzerkampfabzeichen

— Silber —

verliehen.

Rgt.Gef.Std.20.April 1943

SS-Sturmbannführer und Kommandeur

Certificate accompanying the Panzer Badge awarded to Oberschütze Adolf Albers, 5th Company, 3rd SS Panzer Regiment Totenkopf.

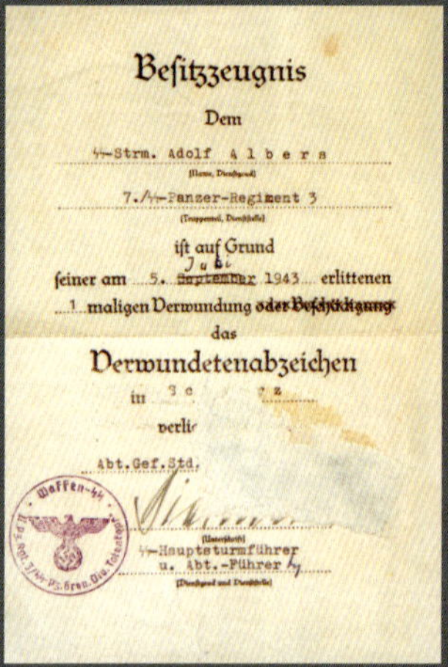

Besitzzeugnis

Dem

SS-Strm. Adolf Albers

7./SS-Panzer-Regiment 3

ist auf Grund

seiner am 5. Juli 1943 erlittenen

1 maligen Verwundung

das

Verwundetenabzeichen

in

verli

Abt.Gef.Std.

SS-Hauptsturmführer u. Abt.-Führer

Certificate accompanying the Wound Badge in black awarded to Adolf Albers.

Oskar Katzer, a close friend of Albers' in 5th Company.

being surrounded. Everyone was nervous. The next evening, we received the order to attack. We, the last two remaining tanks, had to cover the sides of the road while the troops made good their escape.

The retreat restarted on the evening of March 28,1944 and after a few hours' halt during the night, resumed at first light.

Still fatigued, I travelled outside the tank for a while so the cold could wake me up. We came to a valley and passed through a village, under fire from the hills on either side, with Russian infantrymen bustling through the scrub. Then they attacked. Bullets ricocheted off the tanks—time for me to get back in! I did so, as we turned to meet the enemy. We gave them everything we had, advancing without infantry support. Our efforts were in vain—despite firing on them non-stop, the Russians quickly overwhelmed us. The loader ejected one of the shells he had loaded without firing it: now was not the time for the crew to panic! Our dog was on board too, and he threw himself into my lap because shells were falling all around us, and he was terrified. He stuck his head out through the hatch, and it was lucky for him that he did because soon afterward, there was a loud thud, and thick smoke invaded the tank. The engine had caught fire, likely hit by a Molotov cocktail. The driver reacted quickly and reversed the tank back 300 meters in a whirlwind of smoke and flame, hooting defiantly as he did so. We would have to get out of the tank in a sea of Russians, but another tank came back to cover us, drawing enemy fire which gave us a chance to make a run for it. Then that tank broke down, and we had to scuttle it. Now there were ten of us, on foot, fleeing in a hail of bullets, hotly pursued by hordes of Soviet soldiers. I had breathed in too much smoke in the tank, and was struggling to run. I stumbled the last few meters to the safety of our lines. Breathless, we saw the last two tanks of the 3rd SS Panzer Regiment Totenkopf burning like torches in the lines now occupied by the Russians.

Weber spent a few days in hospital due to smoke inhalation, then rejoined the regiment, which was crossing Romania by train, then stationed in Bacau,

A Hauptsturmführer from the tank regiment wearing a number of decorations, including the Iron Cross 1st class and the Hitlerjugend badge. The Totenkopf death's head is on his collar.

Karl Heinz Lorenz (right) in his black uniform and Panzer Badge. He is also wearing the Iron Cross 2nd class ribbon, and the death's head insignia on his collar.

awaiting new panzers from Germany. They spent a few weeks training, and once two new tanks arrived they could train the new recruits to fill the vacancies in the crews. Shooting could only be practiced once or twice a week due to ammunition shortages. Then on July 9, the unit was entrained, without tanks as far as they could tell, and dispatched to Poland.

> After eight days travelling through the most magnificent scenery, we arrived at Zadworzany, near Sokolka.
>
> The Russians continued their offensive, giving us no quarter, pushing us a little farther back every day. We were the only company in the regiment that had not received its tanks, and we found ourselves fighting as infantry. The 1st Battalion, 3rd SS Panzer Regiment, which had been in Grafenwöhr during fall the previous year, had received its new Panther tanks (Panzer Vs), and was fully up to strength with four companies. Finally, after a bitter battle with a band of Russian partisans, we received our brand-new Panzer IVs, equipped with 7.5-cm KwK 40 guns.
>
> Now we were ready for the next attack, on the outskirts of Wolomin, which had thankfully been evacuated by the civilian residents. While waiting for orders, we caught a pig and butchered it, ready to cook, but we had to leave it behind and get back to work, which lasted late into the night. It was 0400 by the time we had a break. The other crews caught pigs too, and we had some good meals out of them. Not far from the house where we were staying, was a beautiful lake, where we bathed in the mornings and evenings, sunbathing on the narrow stretch of beach. We were pretty content, but the front always loomed, and it was now approaching fast. One day, Soviet artillery fired into the town, catching us by surprise while we were swimming.

On August 18, 1944, the Russians broke through our lines in the neighboring town of Klembow, and we were called in as reinforcements. The sun was beaming down on us as we approached the enemy. Mortar shells fell here and there. After passing through a forest, we hit the open road, raising clouds of dust as we made for Klembow. Russian fighter-bombers, like the [Allied] "Jabos" in Normandy, harassed us, but with less accuracy than they had shown in France. Sudden bursts from Stalin's organs decreased visibility to almost zero, as clouds of dust and earth filled the air. It was a glimpse of what lay ahead. We found the breakthrough point and entered the town under an artillery barrage. The enemy was evidently not short of ammunition.

We took shelter in the ruins of a house until the Soviet barrage stopped, several hours later, after nightfall. Several houses were in flames, illuminating the village and the nearby forest. At dawn, the hellish bombardment resumed. First, the mortars, then the large-caliber guns. The noise was so overwhelming we thought the Russian soldiers must be deaf, if they had not been after last night's horrors. At least, I thought, their eardrums would burst. For hours, we huddled into ourselves, trying to protect ourselves from the frightening din. Fortunately, none of our panzers was hit. Some of the houses escaped intact as well, and these structures shielded us from the worst of the shrapnel. Around noon, a lull in the action made us brave enough to poke our heads outside and assess the damage.

Nurses and patients pose for a group photograph at a *Lazarett*, a field hospital. One patient is a Totenkopf Rottenführer wearing the armband and several decorations and ribbons.

In Profile:
Panzer VI "Tiger"

A Panzer VI "Tiger" of the 9th (Heavy) Company, 3rd SS Panzer Regiment. This is the second tank of the second platoon. Note the pieces of track on the side of the turret, as additional armor plating. The fearful 8.8-cm gun on this panzer would prove to be the most destructive of the war; it was also mounted on the Tiger II and the highly successful Jagdpanther tank destroyer.

This Tiger from the Heavy Company, 3rd SS Panzer Regiment, is receiving a coat of white paint for the winter conditions on the steppes.

This Tiger, also from the Heavy Company, 3rd SS Panzer Regiment, appears to have just been hauled out of the mud, judging by the tow cable attached to the front.

That evening, our tank—number 531—was ordered back to the front line to collect the wounded and bring them back to camp. The drive was dreadful, very difficult, and when we arrived at the front, we found only the dead. The infantry had suffered enormous losses. On our return, we were targeted by several Russian antitank guns. No matter where we were or how we positioned ourselves, the shells still found us. They must have had someone spotting up a tree or on a rooftop—it was the only way they could have targeted us so accurately. Later that evening, we attacked the tree line at the edge of the forest, the most likely area for artillery forward observers. The Russians fought back, of course, and during the attack we were hit by an antitank gun, which destroyed a rear track wheel and shattered a leaf spring. However, we somehow managed to bring back the wounded and leave them to the care of the medics before driving to the repair shop. The speed with which our tank was fixed is testament to the skill of the mechanics, as we were action-ready again in next to no time. A few quieter days followed, with little to trouble us but the inevitable artillery fire.

Next, we were sent to a new position, where we would replace the Panther tanks that had stabilized the front in that sector. *It should be calm there*, we thought. And it was calm when we arrived; we settled in, digging ourselves a big hole and parking our tank above it, a cozy spot all said and done.

The next morning, our illusion of calm was shattered by a terrible artillery barrage. It was so intense it shook the earth; we were convinced that we were about to be attacked by the Russians. After two hours of waiting, at around 0600, the firing stopped, but no attack materialized. We did, however, encounter a Landser [a private soldier in the Heer], who told us he was an artillery VB [scout] and asked us what we thought of his shooting. The moron made some boast about hitting the Russians where it hurt most. I almost felt sorry for him when we showed him just how wrong he'd been and he could only blush and apologize for using up so much ammunition for nothing. We disregarded the whole awkward encounter, and sent him on his way.

A Panther from the 4th Company abandoned on the battlefield following engine problems. It has been sabotaged by its crew lest it fall into Russian hands.

A crisp photograph of a Panzer III from the 3rd SS Panzer Regiment Totenkopf with its commander in the turret. Note the death's head insignia on the rear of the tank.

> Meanwhile, Soviet fighter aircraft reappeared to harass our infantry holding the village behind us. I had gotten back into the tank and was reading something when I heard a loud noise. A tree had fallen onto the tank, hitting our commander, Oberscharführer Horst Marx, who was in the turret. He collapsed into the tank with a stream of blood, dead. The offending tree had been hit by a shell, which uprooted it, turning it into a deadly projectile. Our loader was also injured, but it was minor, and the rest of us were unharmed. We laid the commander's body in a shallow trench next to the tank; we were not allowed to leave our positions in case the Soviets attacked again.

That evening a new commander arrived, and they were instructed to move forward as a minefield had been laid behind them, and beyond that was an antitank trench. They were advised how to cross these obstacles in case they had to retreat.

> The next day, we received a nasty shock. The units supposed to be supporting our flanks had disappeared during the night, withdrawing without waiting for orders: it wouldn't be difficult for the Russians to flank us now, given the gaps left on each side by our dear friends from the Heer!
>
> The quiet didn't last long—it never does—and soon we heard noises in the wheat fields in front of us. Row upon row of Russian infantry were advancing mechanically toward us, oblivious to their surroundings, as if on exercise. They veered left toward the village. It was clear by this point that they hadn't spotted us hiding at the edge of the forest. Seemingly without encountering any problems or obstacles, the enemy infantry reached the village. We did nothing to give away our position; we knew all hell was about to be unleashed.

That evening, the ground shook and the sky was obscured by a massive cloud of dust raised by the hordes of Soviet tanks now converging on the village. We just watched it happen. We were only three tanks, so what could we do against thirty?

Suddenly, three enemy Sherman tanks emerged from a position between two houses and started heading for us. After a brief pause to assess the threat, we opened fire, and all three burst into flames. Unfortunately, this drew the attention of the other enemy tanks, as those closest to the edge of the village attacked us from behind. I managed to destroy one and my comrades another, but we were at risk of being surrounded. The infantrymen accompanying us joined us in our retreat—but once we reached the minefield, there was no sign of the "safe path" we'd been instructed to follow. I was stunned when one young soldier stepped forward and volunteered to find a path through the deadly trap. Somehow this brave young man managed to find a way, with only his wits, and courage, to guide him. And, thank God, none of our three tanks hit a mine, though it was painfully slow-going. We managed to get past the antitank trenches just fine, but then we were faced with getting through the forest. We could hear Russian tanks moving all around us, and though we fired a few times, I don't think we hit anything. Somehow, we made it back to our lines and the battalion command post, where our other tanks were already parked. Overcome after the trials of the day, we barely managed to replenish our fuel and ammunition before collapsing into our bunks and falling asleep. We had been very lucky.

No sooner had the sun's first rays appeared over the horizon than we received our orders for the day—"we" being two panzers and an infantry unit. When we arrived at our new position, the infantry immediately dug bunkers which they graciously invited us to share. Only the occasional mortar explosion interrupted

A Panzer III crew using a brush to clean the 5-cm gun barrel, in the field.

A Rottenführer from the 3rd SS Panzer Regiment in his black uniform with several decorations and, on his arm, the truck driver's insignia beneath the Totenkopf armband.

For this tank crew it's time for a pork barbecue. Supplies were always sparse and ration deliveries were often late.

the peace that evening. The next day was pretty calm too, allowing us some time to rest and to clear our minds a little. Our bunker was in a garden, and our tank was about 30 meters away, under the shelter of some trees. One of the infantrymen stood guard outside. We were ready for action if needed.

The next night was anything but peaceful. I was on guard duty from 0000 to 0200, and I had just finished my shift when the deafening sound of gunfire filled the air. We didn't know what was happening at first, but then the commander told us to get into our tanks. The Russians had taken a shortcut through a marshy area to reach the garden. Our troops had already dispersed under enemy fire, and were starting to retreat. I grabbed my things and ran to our tank. There was a little moonlight but a thin mist obscured it, casting eerie shadows across the ground. Bullets were flying everywhere, whistling past my head as I ran. I was almost at the tank when I heard someone shout a warning—"*Stoij* "—so I jumped to the side, narrowly avoiding a Russian soldier who didn't see me. We boarded the tank quickly. Only the loader was missing; he had initially mistaken the Russian infantry surrounding us for our own men, and was therefore somewhere behind us. Fortunately, our tank was so well camouflaged that the Russians hadn't seen it. We had to reverse it out of its hiding place, before trying to find the other tank. In the meantime, our loader found us.

It took a long time to find the other tank. The crew, upon hearing the news of what had happened, decided it was best for us to stick together. Now we had our tanks, we were finally able to counterattack and destroy the morning assailants. As the fog cleared, we reduced the Russian attack to nothing. The survivors fled back to their lines, even faster than they had arrived.

We moved again soon after and found ourselves settled in a defensive position on the outskirts of Radzymin, waiting for a Russian attack on the town. Two kilometers into the forest, enemy tanks were waiting. We watched

Unterscharführer Siegfried Kruger, a Panther crewmember in the 3rd SS Panzer Regiment Totenkopf, poses for a photo dated October 18, 1944. Note that, in addition to the Totenkopf armband, he is also wearing the badge awarded to those who fought at Demjansk.

In Profile:

Unterscharführer Ernst Walter Kirsch

October 21, 1921–March 16, 2006

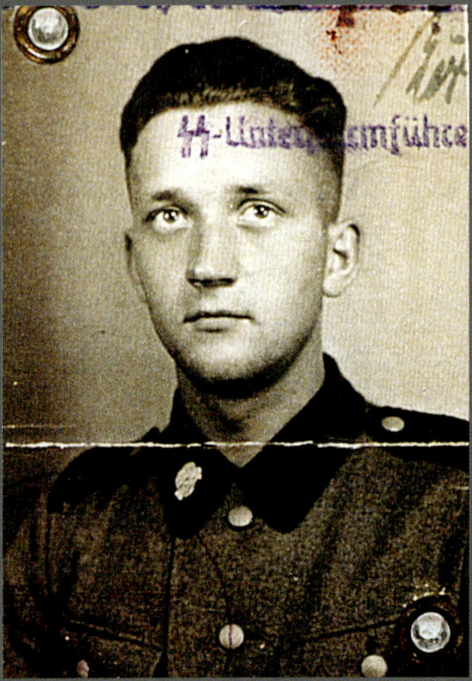

A photograph from Ernst Walter Kirsch's *Soldbuch*, taken at the time he joined the Totenkopf Division.

Ernst Walter Kirsch as an Oberscharführer, his face marked by the harshness of combat.

SS

Schirrmeister-K

Der SS-Rottf. Kirsch Ernst

geb 21.10.21 in Fürstenstein

hat die Prüfung als

Schirrmeister-K

bestanden

Wien, den 28.5.1942

Der Kommandeur

der Kraftfahrtechnischen Lehranstalt der SS

SS-Standartenführer

Ernst Walter Kirsch undertook an advanced training course to become a tank mechanic—this is his diploma, which he received in Vienna.

Ernst Walter Kirsch, helmeted, as a Sturmmann.

Ernst Walter Kirsch.

An excellent photograph of Unterscharführer Ernst Walter Kirsch in his black uniform with a pistol in his belt.

Nur gültig für die Dauer des Dienstverhältnisses
bei der SS. (Bei der Entlassung abzugeben.)

Fahrlehrerschein

für

den Ernst Kirsch
(Vor- und Zuname)

Dienstgrad: SS-Unterscharf.

Einheit: 5./SS-Kraftf.Ers.Abt.

geboren am 21. Oktober 1921

in Fürstenstein/Passau

Der SS-Unterscharf.
(Dienstgrad, Zuname)

Ernst Kirsch

erhält hiermit die Erlaubnis zur Ausbildung von Kraftfahrzeugführern der SS auf Kraftfahrzeugen mit Antrieb durch

Verbrennungsmaschine

der Klasse I u.II

Dieser Schein ist bei Lehr- und Prüfungsfahrten mitzuführen; er verliert bei Entziehung des Führerscheines ohne weiteres seine Gültigkeit.

Berlin, den 4.November 1942

SS-Führungshauptamt
i. A.
SS-Obersturmbannführer
u. Kommandeur

Liste Nr. 3/11/42

A rare full and half-track vehicle driving instructor's license belonging to Ernst Walter Kirsch.

them all day while listening in, futilely, on their communications, which we did not understand. Some other tanks joined us, as well as Sturmgeschütz IIIs and three Tigers.

The night was quiet, disturbed only by the sound of our own tanks changing positions, though we had no idea at the time what that entailed. The morning sun shone light on the matter: our tank and another were the only ones left in position! The day was already scorching hot, and the Russian attack came early. A blanket of artillery shells fell on the town, as swarms of cheering Russian infantrymen attacked our troops, who were forced to retreat. We also had to retreat, or else be surrounded. We ended in up in the center of the town, where two Tigers were in battle with two heavy JS-1s. The Tigers, too, had to retreat.

We were preparing to leave the town when we received radio orders to stay where we were, and that armored reinforcements were on their way. We didn't believe it, but orders are orders. We were driving down a narrow street when our companion panzer was hit and exploded. Even its ammunition exploded. The radio operator and driver were able to escape, but with severe burns on their arms and faces.

The enemy infantry seemed to be growing stronger, and were now on the streets. We fired everything we had at them to hold them off as we made our escape. We arrived at the command post where we thought we might find the promised reinforcements. They weren't there.

This captured T-34 has been adopted by the 3rd SS Panzer Regiment Totenkopf. A Heer photographer has climbed on top of it.

We retreated again, to well-established positions that the infantry were already occupying. For our part, our positions were three kilometers to the rear, in Pustelnik forest. There, we had some time to put our tank in order. We dug a trench that we stuffed with straw and then moved the tank over it, to protect us from Russian "Jabos" and artillery shrapnel.

By September 10, 1944, our company was finally up to strength again, so the Russian artillery picked a "good" day to target us. The forest seemed to burst open with explosions. The hole we had made under our tank had room for ten men, but it was quite shallow, so we suffered a little more than expected from the pressure of the Soviet artillery. Suddenly, there was a loud noise and I felt like my right thigh had been hit by a baseball bat. Dust and cordite filled the trench, making it hard to breathe. Immediately, I crawled out of the hole to make a dash to the cover of the second tank. Halfway there, I collapsed, my leg no longer responding. I had to drag myself the rest of the way through a storm of explosions and shrapnel. I made it to cover under the second tank, where two of my comrades were already sheltering. We were stuck there until the bombardment eventually ended. Of the ten men who had been under our tank, nine were wounded—the tenth had been killed. The tank tracks had taken a direct hit, flinging shrapnel and debris under the tank, and we were all wounded because we hadn't dug our hole deep enough. I had a large piece of metal stuck in my right thigh.

Unterscharführer Kurt Söhrmann at his radio post in Panther number 101, commanded by Erwin Meierdress. The *zimmerit* is clearly visible. This photo was taken at Neustadt, Poland, in December 1944.

Hungary

On December 25, 1944, the Totenkopf received urgent orders to deploy to Hungary. Budapest was encircled by the Soviets and 95,000 German and Hungarian troops were surrounded. On January 1, 1945, the Wiking and Totenkopf divisions launched Operation *Konrad* on the Biscke–Budapest Line but it was repulsed by the Red Army. On January 7, Operation *Konrad II* was launched and although panzergrenadiers of the Wiking Division penetrated Budapest's northern suburbs, the Waffen-SS were overextended and fell back. Operation *Konrad III* was launched on January 20, but Budapest capitulated on February 13. It seemed that Hungary would become the Totenkopf's graveyard.

Unterscharführer Kurt Sörhmann was a radio operator in Panther I01 in the 1st Battalion, 3rd SS Panzer Regiment. Having joined the Waffen-SS in 1942 he was initially the radio operator in the commander's tank. In October 1943, the 1st Battalion was reformed at Grafenwöhr in Germany, and was then sent northwest of Warsaw. There Söhrmann served as head of radio communications in Erwin Meierdress's tank.

On the train carrying their Panthers to Hungary, these three members of the 3rd SS Panzer Regiment Totenkopf are wearing reversible winter camouflage uniforms.

Cattle wagons and flatbeds were the most commonly used mode of rail transport to move troops from one front to another.

> We were there for quite some time when we were ordered to the station for transfer to Budapest as a matter of urgency to break the encirclement around the Hungarian capital. After passing through Bromberg, Posen, Breslau, and Vienna, we reached Komárom, on December 28, 1944, and disembarked. We were stationed near Raab. Most of the 3rd SS Panzer Regiment ended up in a Hungarian barracks. We had at our disposal 16 Panzer IVs, 29 Panzer Vs (Panther) and 11 Panzer VIs (Tiger).
>
> We celebrated the new year with large amounts of alcohol; the group's informal leitmotiv was: "Enjoy the war, peace will be terrible." Fiery artillery explosions lit up the sky in place of fireworks when the clock struck midnight, aimed eastward.
>
> At 0215, the offensive on Budapest began, but the 3rd SS Panzer Regiment "T" was not as yet involved in the action. It was -3 degrees. On January 2, we started the day by repainting our tanks with a mixture of white chalk, which we applied with brushes. The fresh morning air did a great job waking us up for the offensive. Only half our forces were available as, out of 77 rail convoys, only 51 had arrived. And that was just the 3rd SS Panzer Division. For the 5th SS Panzer Division Wiking, only 28 of 87—a third of its strength—had made it! The other divisions were in similar positions.

Fritz Edelman recalled that at the end of December 1944, 5th Company was based at Świerże, near Nasielsk, and had only eight operational Panzer IV tanks. Weber remembers that according to their orders, they would be spending Christmas there, and so they made preparations, decorating a large room in an old factory, and writing up a special newsletter. The party began at 1900 on Christmas Eve. The tankers enjoyed two hours of great fun until "the alarm was sounded at 2100 as the enemy, who did not celebrate Christmas, had begun

In Profile:
Unterscharführer Kurt Söhrmann
December 20, 1922–July 12, 2006

Unterscharführer Kurt Söhrmann working on the engine of one of the unit's vehicles.

An interesting photo of Kurt Söhrmann, here with the rank of Sturmmann, and wearing the Iron Cross 2nd class ribbon, the Wound Badge, and the Panzer Badge, alongside the Hitler Youth Sports Association insignia. He is also wearing the Totenkopf armband and, just above that, the lightning bolt of the Signals Corps (Nachrichten).

Members of Kurt Söhrmann's Panther crew in their reversible winter clothing sit behind their tank, the exhaust pipes of which are clearly visible.

Unterscharführer Kurt Söhrmann at his radio post in the Panther. Note the *zimmerit*.

Above: An excellent photograph of Kurt Söhrmann in his camouflage overalls.

Below: Unterscharführer Kurt Söhrmann, in his padded winter camouflage outfit, stands in front of his panzer.

Sepp Hirsch (left) and Kurt Söhrmann.

Kurt Söhrmann, at his radio post, calmly smoking a cigarette during a lull in the fighting. This photo was taken when he was still a Rottenführer, in September 1944 in Poland. Note his camouflage cap and the *zimmerit* applied to the tank.

Unterscharführer Kurt Söhrmann jauntily smoking a cigar given to him by his friend Schorsch.

an attack. In a very short time, everything was cleared, our packs prepared and brought into the tanks. We were very upset that our festivities had been cut short." On December 26, the company was loaded onto trains to be sent to Hungary. "The train ride was a long one so we entertained ourselves with a few bottles of wine that we'd recovered from the Christmas party."

> On December 29 we arrived at Acs, where we disembarked and drove to the front. Despite everything, we'd planned another small party to celebrate the New Year. Of course, we should have known better. On December 31, we were ordered to advance to start positions for an attack that would begin the next day. At 2200 we set off, and shortly before midnight, arrived at our destination. Despite our proximity to the front, we rang in the New Year by setting off some flares. Ivan was very quiet—the sound of our vehicles must have worried him.

Edelman recalled the journey to Hungary:

> We passed Bromberg, Posen, Breslau, and Vienna, and ended the journey at Györ, Hungary. Our quarters were at Szöny, and our mission was to break the encirclement of the German troops in Budapest, where several Waffen-SS cavalry divisions were also located.
>
> On the evening of January 1, 1945, we departed, in two stages, and reached Paks on the Danube, from where we spearheaded the attack. Obersturmführer Wenke led the battle group and Unterscharführer Bepp Windisch commanded tank number 501.
>
> Another attack was launched the next evening, led this time by Oberscharführer Griego. Advancing in a large curved formation, we avoided fire from artillery and antitank guns by constantly adjusting our speed. From there, we organized the

Two trains on the way to the front: on the left Panthers, and on the right Tigers, all from the 3rd SS Panzer Regiment.

attack as in the good old days, attacking the village of Bajot en masse with all the firepower we possessed. We passed through it and continued until we were stopped in our tracks by a minefield, and had to call in the pathfinders.

When we arrived at the village of Bajna, Russian tanks started shooting at us. To our left, Oschs. Griego's tank was hit. I fired back, setting a thatched roof alight that lit up the area and gave us a better view of the enemy positions. I destroyed a tank with two shells; our gunner, Rottenführer Grimminger, performed brilliantly.

We moved into the village, passing a knocked-out Soviet assault gun with its imposing 122-mm barrel. A little farther on, we came to a crossroads where some T-34s and JS-1s ambushed us from behind some houses, welcoming us with some large-caliber shells. At daybreak, the infantry was still fighting in the streets. A Tiger tried to break through the enemy barrage and had to make a speedy retreat when it was targeted by Russian gunners. The same thing happened to a Panther. Obersturmführer Wenke came over and asked if any of our panzers were equipped with radios that could contact the Luftwaffe. We found the right frequency and managed to request air support. The pilots asked us to send up orange flares when they arrived overhead. Ten minutes later, two Ju 88s appeared, we sent up the flares and our aviator comrades kindly cleared the crossroads for us.

We continued our advance through Czomor and Szambek. After heavy losses in bitter fighting against forces much larger than ours, we were withdrawn from

Another view of the rail convoys, Panthers and Tigers from the Heavy Company, 3rd SS Panzer Regiment.

In Profile:
Panzer V "Panther"

The beautiful lines of a Panzer V "Panther." This one is wearing an exotic camouflage scheme that proved extremely efficient. The Panther was the more modern replacement of the ubiquitous Panzer IV and was regarded as the best medium tank of the war. With its long-barreled 7.5-cm cannon, it was capable of destroying most Allied types, especially since the range of the gun exceeded that of most enemy tanks. As such, Panther panzer crews tended to accumulate high kill rates.

An imposing view of Kurt Arp's Panther, 3rd SS Panzer Regiment Totenkopf.

A Panther pauses during an advance next to a Soviet *izba*. The panzer commander is conferring with a panzergrenadier officer, from the same Totenkopf Division.

the front and transported by train to Komárom. From there, we were driven to Veszprém to carry out an attack on Stuhlweissenburg. It was our last fight: 501 hit a mine and was badly damaged, and our driver Franz Käsmacher was killed. I was forced to surrender, and was sent to a prisoner-of-war camp.

Unterscharführer Kurt Sörhmann recalled that the 1st Battalion, 3rd SS Panzer Regiment, started by advancing along the banks of the Danube:

> The first battle took place at Duna-Szt-Miklos, where the Russians had established a stronghold.
>
> Our command tank was waiting for orders, and to be joined by our leader, Erwin Meierdress. As the radio operator, I was in contact with the regimental command post, as well as that of the panzergrenadiers. Our driver, Sepp Hirsch, let the engine run to warm the cabin. Our loader and second radio operator, Sturmmann Sepp Tittel, made contact with the company commander and the platoon commanders. Our gunner, Obersturmführer Alfred Quilitz, was doing nothing at that moment. Finally, our commander got on board. After asking us if everything was OK, he gave the driver the order to move out. The few Tigers in the division were at the head of the column.
>
> At around 0500, the attack began. We were on the outskirts of Dunaalmas, where the Russians had formed a barrage with 18 T-34s and antitank guns. The Tigers' 8.8-cm guns lit up everything they pointed their barrels at, all the while being hit themselves. The leading Tiger was stopped, but the others continued

A 3rd SS Panzer Division Panther—likely returning to base to replenish fuel and ammunition—passing some Totenkopf panzergrenadiers.

under the guidance of Obersturmführer Scheinhofer. Flurries of incendiary rounds enveloped the antitank guns, killing the crews. One after the other, the Tigers were stopped, and we ended up taking the lead in the assault. Following directly behind us was the Panther of Obersturmführer Strobl, the company adjutant. It was still dark and we hadn't fired a round yet. Suddenly, the commander ordered the driver to stop and then hurried out of the tank. We asked each other what was going on; Obersturmführer Quilitz explained that Meierdress wanted to discuss the situation with the panzergrenadier commanders, Hauptsturmführer Endress and Hauptsturmführer Frommhagen. Then, Meierdress returned, and we checked our watch. It was 0645. The Sturmbannführer ordered the driver to continue.

Shortly thereafter, there was a deafening noise, a big red flash and a wave of heat. Outside, the turret was turned to 1 o'clock; it was blocking my hatch, so I had to take the whole thing apart to get out. Once I had done so, I dived straight into a trench, where the driver Sepp Hirsch was already taking cover. The panzer was still moving, so Sepp climbed out of the trench and jumped onto the tank, clinging to the barrel, to turn off the ignition. Everyone in the turret was dead. Sepp and I were both wounded; I had severe burns that would lead to a long stay in hospital.

Here's what happened: our Panther had stopped behind a house, but a Russian assault gun had spotted it and was waiting for us to start moving again to shoot at us. He had plenty of time to focus his aim, and he hit the Panther on the right side, just under a piece of track we had hung there. The news of Meierdress's death spread like wildfire, as he had been very popular among the men. The Russian assault gun was destroyed seconds later by Panther I03, whose gunner was none other than Unterscharführer Kurt Arp.

Unterscharführer Kurt Arp investigates a problem with his panzer.

It took quite some time for the Totenkopf Division to overcome the Russians, as the enemy had established strong defensive positions at Dunaalmas, near the railway. However, one by one, the Russian tanks were destroyed, including seven that the "Eicke" Regiment panzergrenadiers took out with Panzerfausts.

The same day, after the battlefield had been cleared, Unterscharführer Sepp Hirsch brought back our Panther, with the bodies of the three dead crewmembers still in the turret. We carefully brought down the bodies of our commander and two comrades, and said farewell to them with tears in our eyes. At least we had the memories of our New Year's celebrations as some comfort. The commander's body was driven to Vienna, where it was buried alongside that of the famous pilot Walter Nowotny.

Walter Weber recalled that:

At around 2000 on January 1, 1945, the entire 3rd SS Panzer Regiment attacked. We might not have been as formidable as we had been when the regiment was first created, but it was still a proud moment when we were all assembled. The 1st Battalion, equipped with their Panthers, attacked alongside the Tigers of the Heavy Company. We followed them and, sometime later, took the lead. The attack went like a dream. Our path took us along the Danube, so we were able to move with relative ease. On the opposite bank, the infantry was advancing too. A few kilometers away, the 5th SS Panzer Division Wiking was also advancing. We were due to link up with them outside Budapest. Moonlight bleached out the countryside, already whitened by a thin layer of snow, which our tanks handled easily. We halted in a large field, waiting for the Panthers to begin the attack a little way ahead of us. Without artillery preparation, we had to move fast to benefit from the element of surprise. Only when we reached the first Russian lines would things really get going. We heard the Panthers ahead, and set off toward the city.

The Russians defended like men possessed and before we knew it, we were taking casualties. We halted for a few moments outside a village, before following the Panthers in. At first light, we captured the village. We halted again, and the Panthers again went ahead. We were surprised when Hungarian civilians began emerging from their homes and cellars, asking us if we were German, because they weren't sure. We assured them that we were, then resumed our advance to catch up with the Panthers. Hungarians were gathering in the streets, elated at being freed from the Russians, bringing us food and showering our tanks with flowers.

That evening, we made so much progress that we took the lead from the 1st Battalion (Panthers) who had run out of ammo. Following a protective ridge for a few hundred meters, we then moved onto flatter ground, within range of Russian antitank guns. Several shells fell nearby, but it was still relatively calm. We veered off the main road and drove through the adjoining fields at full speed, following the slightly uneven terrain until we arrived in some gardens where the few enemy troops we encountered fled. As darkness fell, we reached the village of Bajot with the rest of the battalion's armored vehicles.

At 0100, we attacked again, our panzer in the van. The road stretched out in front of us in the moonlight, hills to both left and right. There were almost definitely some Russians hiding out in those hills, ready to throw us a little welcoming party. Still, at least it wasn't raining. A minefield laid by the Russians hindered us somewhat and we wasted a lot of time getting past it. The calm

A wrecked sidecar is stripped for parts.

surprised us, and didn't bode well for the days to come. Bajna appeared in front of us. We stopped and fired on the houses at the entrance to the village with our tank guns and machine guns. That was a rude awakening for the villagers! The thatched roofs lit up like torches as the enemy guns responded. There were explosions everywhere; tankers and infantrymen alike went down in the firestorm. We were slowly able to seize the main road through the village and move forward. We plunged deeper into the village, fighting for every meter. Arriving near the church, we saw a column of Russian vehicles driving past. Shells burst in front of us, on the road, against houses, making an infernal noise.

Two enemy tanks were blocking the path of an entire panzer regiment in those narrow streets. In the early morning, we called for reinforcements in the form of three Tigers to help clear this nest of resistance. They arrived, protected by their heavy armor, thundering through the streets. The commanders were halfway out of their turrets, asking us where the target was. We told them it was at the church, and they filed off, one after the other, toward the Russians. The first Tiger had just come into range of the church when a shell took off its turret! The second was hit with a large-caliber shell in its tracks, and was terribly damaged, which caused trouble when it tried to retreat. The two Russian T-85s were not playing around. The third Tiger advanced too, firing a few rounds but without much success, all the while being targeted itself. It retreated before the Russians had a chance to do too much damage. The commander of the third tank told us later that the two Russian tanks had been very well positioned behind the church. The streets adjacent were all within their range, but it was difficult to see the Russian tanks properly and therefore the Tigers couldn't get a clear shot at them.

Evening fell, and the two tanks were still standing. They hadn't moved an inch, and were still firing antitank and high-explosive shells that wreaked havoc on the houses and the roads, not to mention our eardrums. As night fell, we set up camp in a quieter area to regroup. The two tanks were, in fact, destroyed during the night by infantrymen approaching from a lateral angle. The next morning, around 0400, while it was still dark, we resumed our journey, and drove past the two smoking wrecks on our way out of the village.

Once back in the countryside, we found ourselves being fired on from a farmstead just off the road. We returned fire, and soon heard the sound of a tank retreating. It was troubling to see how many tanks and antitank guns the Russians had deployed against us. It was easy for them to delay our advance by using every house, every farmstead, as a base of resistance, knowing that we, with our tanks, had to take the main road. And once they had done their damage, they could easily withdraw to other buildings farther back, causing us many losses.

We advanced a little more, then stopped to wait for the infantry to catch up. We were on the right side of the road, in second position, while the leading tank was in the middle of the road, observing the area ahead. The commander had just fired a white flare to illuminate the terrain around us, but he'd also illuminated his own tank in doing so. A loud band and bright flash followed, leaving us with no doubt that the leading tank had been hit. The tank commander's leg was blown off but he managed to get out only by throwing himself onto the ground. The gunner, driver and radio operator were also able to get out, and carried their commander to a nearby trench. The loader died at his post. We reversed our tank so we wouldn't be targeted next.

This T-34 has been destroyed by a shell from Kurt Söhrmann's Panther.

In Profile: Sturmbannführer Erwin Meierdress

December 11, 1916–January 4, 1945

Born in Wesel, Erwin Meierdress was awarded the Knight's Cross on March 13, 1942 while serving as commander of the Totenkopf Sturmgeschütz Battery, and then the Oak Leaves on October 12, 1943. He was killed in action at Dunaalmas, Hungary, and was buried in Vienna.

Official photo of Hauptsturmführer Erwin Meierdress with the Knight's Cross with Oak Leaves.

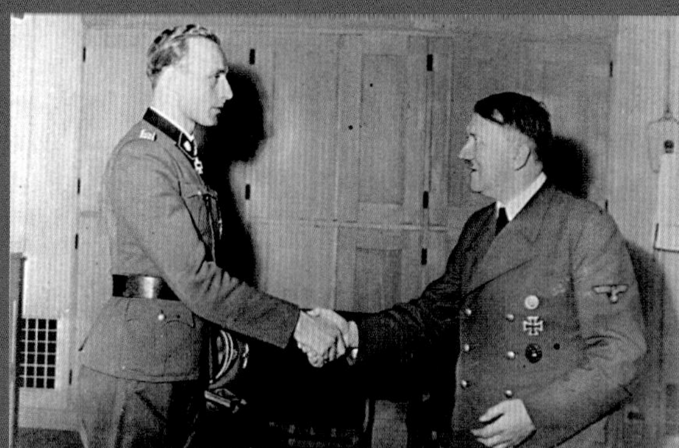

Erwin Meierdress, receiving the Oak Leaves for his Knight's Cross, shakes hands with Adolf Hitler.

Hauptsturmführer Erwin Meierdress in his black tanker's uniform and RK with two fellow officers. He commanded the 1st Battalion, 3rd SS Panzer Regiment Totenkopf.

Sturmbannführer Erwin Meierdress in front of a destroyed T-34.

Erwin Meierdress, in a light shirt, discussing a Panther tank with fellow tankers.

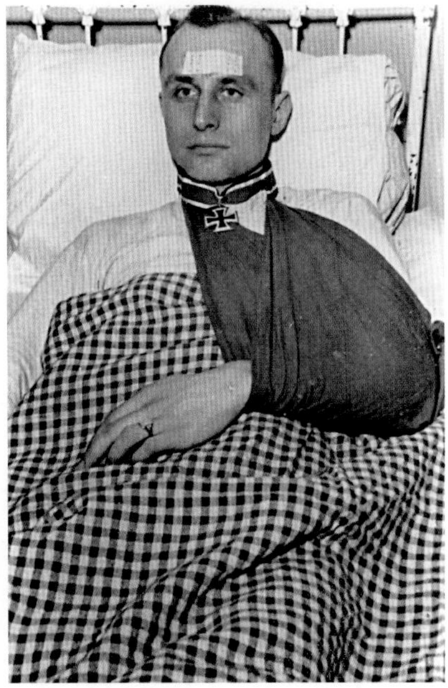

Wounded but still wearing his Knight's Cross, Erwin Meierdress pictured here in hospital.

Erwin Meierdress after his injury, convalescing at home with his parents, poses here with his father.

Back on the Eastern Front, Erwin Meierdress confers with his officers.

Sturmbannführer Erwin Meierdress with all his decorations.

A young Rottenführer of the 3rd SS Panzer Regiment Totenkopf. He has the death's head insignia on his collar, but no military decorations.

The sun was rising, and we were able to make out a Russian assault gun, more from the smoke emanating from its barrel than from the weapon itself. We dispatched an antitank round, which ricocheted off its armor. We followed it up with a hollow-charge round, which hit the mark and blew up the gun.

We did not move from our position, as a group of eight to ten large-caliber JS-1 tanks were out on a reconnaissance mission, and we did not want to draw attention to ourselves. But soon we were deployed elsewhere where the action was hotter. When we arrived, we found ourselves facing off against a group of heavy JS-1 tanks. It was going to be a fierce fight. Unfortunately, the unthinkable happened and our engine wouldn't start. We tried over and over, but we couldn't get it to fire. A Panther moved up alongside, firing at the Russian tanks. The shells had little effect, as the heavy armor of the JS-1 protected it perfectly. Its own 122-mm rounds were landing closer and closer to the Panther. That poor crew! What would they have done if one of those shells had hit them? Thankfully, luck was on their side, as the pride of the regiment, two Tigers, came up. The commander of the Heavy Company, Obersturmführer Gerhard Wenke himself, was in the second Tiger, and swiftly brought it into position. Within moments he had assessed the situation and before we knew it, shells were blasting out of the long 8.8-cm barrel. Plumes of smoke spiraled skyward as the Russian tanks exploded, hit by the Tiger's rounds.

It was at this moment that our airborne tank destroyers appeared, and we directed them toward the enemy, making short work of them with their 3.7-cm guns. Clouds of black smoke filled the air as tank after tank was destroyed, much to our relief. We had been watching the fighting for some time when our engine finally spluttered into life. We had no idea what had happened to it; the main thing was that it was working again. That evening, we returned to the village to replenish our ammunition and fuel, but as the gasoline hadn't arrived, we had a brief respite. The next day, at 1200, we were finally able to refuel and leave. Our panzer regiment had fought throughout the night, but had suffered heavy losses. As we advanced, we passed blackened hulks, the battlefield a tank graveyard, Russian and German alike.

After presenting ourselves to the commander, we found ourselves once again at the front of our platoon for a new attack. We accelerated across a field and arrived at the top of a ridge, our appearance heralded by shots of all calibers coming from every part of the Soviet line. Then the Stalin's organs joined in, and the explosions began to creep closer. There were four of us panzers when the attack began, and one had already been hit, unable to move as its wheels had been shattered. In front of us, a village was shrouded in smoke created by our artillery, allowing us to enter unmolested. We sent a few shells into the hills, from where the occasional shot was still coming. The infantry, following our lead, cleared the ground of the few remaining Russian troops.

We resumed our position at the head of the platoon, in the third wave behind the Panthers. Once outside the village, the road angled slightly upward, offering us some protection against the enemy and allowing us to advance unseen. As soon as the first tank reached the top of the slope, there was a flash and a loud bang, and there was nothing left but a flaming wreck. We pulled back, zigzagging across the road, and waited for the infantry to arrive, before resuming the attack. Two Panthers, on the right, were tasked with taking out the Russians. Unfortunately, the operation was not successful, and with darkness falling, we decided to take shelter in a village farther back down the road. My tank found cover behind a farmstead, out of sight of the Russians. The night passed without incident.

The next morning, it began to snow, and before we knew it a white blanket covered the landscape. More infantry arrived, and the attack was rescheduled for the next morning. Just before daybreak, the Russians attacked. The infantrymen barely had time to get out of their sleeping holes before fire from light Flak guns forced them back in. Some of them were killed. We wanted to get to our tanks, but the mortar and artillery fire was too heavy. The Russians now knew our position, and were targeting us. The farmstead where we were hidden was soon completely destroyed, but somehow, we all escaped injury. We were finally able to move when the sun went down. We returned to the village, where we linked up with the rest of the panzergrenadiers, and together prepared to launch the next attack during the night.

We slowly drove down the side of the road, through snow-covered fields. The target of our nocturnal attack was the next village, currently in the hands of the Russians. With the help of some flares, we could make out a corn field ahead, but when we turned toward it, we were greeted with a variety of small-arms fire. I could make out some antitanks as well. So that was where the Russians were waiting for us. With our position now given away, the infantry sent up several flares so we could better see the field that was about to become our battleground. As we arrived at the corn field, we stopped to fire on the village with our tank guns and machine guns. The flares had burned out, and darkness enveloped the battlefield. Suddenly, to our left, one of our tanks fired, and a Russian vehicle lit up in flames. The enemy tank had been well camouflaged and was waiting for us to approach it to fire on us. Had we come 50 meters closer, it would have done for us. By now, the gunfire was so intense that to continue advancing would have been suicidal. So, we veered right, avoiding the village and the worst of the shooting. We stopped in an orchard and sent out a reconnaissance party to get a better idea of what was happening. To our left, very close by, an antitank gun was firing incessantly. We could even hear the Russian commander barking out orders and the slamming of the breech and the clinking of the empty cases being ejected. We hadn't picked a great spot for a break—we were right in the middle of a nest of Russian antitank guns!

Slowly and carefully, we withdrew, swinging left, and took cover in the lee of a hill to wait for daybreak.

When dawn broke, we were able to view our surroundings, and were stunned to see a large number of Russian tanks and antitank guns all around us. The Russians were waking up now, too, and soon opened fire on us. We were exposed. Farther down, the road was totally deserted. The Russians were determined, it seemed, to wipe us out, and already a nearby tank had been hit, the shells inside it exploding. I looked back at the empty road and saw eight Russian tanks, one behind the other, driving down it. Apparently, they hadn't spotted us. I made a spur-of-the-moment decision, and shot down the last tank of the column, and

Kurt Arp wrote on the back of this snap: "The road was dusty. We were driving along the edge of a wood."

then the one in the middle. The other panzers, alerted by the noise, joined the fray, and in an instant the eight Russian tanks were nothing but distorted metal and flame. We braced ourselves for a response, but saw just one Russian tank, at the bottom on the hill, which I took care of. If the rest of the day went like this, it would be perfect!

Our tank commander had just been summoned by the company commander outside the tank, and the loader was just taking his place in the turret when a shell hit our right side. At my post at the radio, I could still hear talking through the headset as billows of smoke filled the compartment. My hand was screaming with pain, but I managed to follow my three comrades out of the tank. The driver was still wearing his headset. Luckily, the tank didn't explode. The commander and the company commander appeared to have been slightly wounded. We gathered round to assess the damage. It was a good thing the loader had left his position—had he stayed he would have lost his legs. As it was, he was completely unscathed. As we were all still alive and mostly in one piece, we all piled back into the tank as the driver began to take us back to the repair shop. Even the engine seemed to have had luck on its side, as it was still functioning surprisingly well. The shell had ripped a gash of a meter—a meter!—in the armor on the side of the tank, and the shrapnel would have killed the loader had he been in position. The luck of the warrior! As it was, a piece of metal had hit my hand, which I could no longer feel or move.

This was January 7, 1945, and we were near Zambek, around 15 kilometers from Budapest. On the way to the workshop, we had to take a road along the Danube that was vulnerable to enemy fire, as the enemy had occupied the opposite bank after a counterattack. Many wrecked vehicles already littered the road, making our passage difficult. Under pressure from Russian fire, the driver put his foot down and sped along the icy road. Despite the obstacles and the slippery

A well-camouflaged Totenkopf Panther on the edge of a wood.

surface, he had to keep going as fast as possible. A flash blinded us for a moment, but the shell missed by a few feet. We reached our destination without further incident, and were relieved to find that the area was much quieter. After three days at the workshop, we were able to resume our journey to the front.

With my injury, I should really have left the front but, as there was no transfer possible and as the front had stabilized, I ended up staying with my comrades. We were soon relieved and sent to another hotspot, at Stuhlweissenburg, near Lake Balaton. The next day, we withdrew from Zambek with the rest of the panzer regiment. Once again, we had to take the road along the Danube, which was so dangerous. Fortunately, there was fog that day, making it easier for us to sneak past the Russians without being spotted. At Komárom, our tanks were loaded onto trains to be quickly transported to Lake Balaton and Stuhlweissenburg, where we, alongside a battalion of Royal Tigers (Panzer VIs), would meet a Russian offensive intended to cut off our advance on Budapest where our encircled comrades were waiting for us. What a pleasure it was to see those armored giants ignoring the fire of the Russian antitank guns and destroying them as if swatting flies.

We arrived at Veszprém where, along with some old comrades, we found our "rural" quarters. It was calm there, and we were able to enjoy a brief respite before being thrown back into battle. Hungarian wine flowed freely, and good meat satisfied our hungry bellies. We were stationed in a remote village called Bakonyis-Zentkiralyi, some 30 kilometers from the nearest town. For us, it was like being stationed at the edge of the world. Soon, new crewmembers, just out of school, joined us, and my team returned to its infantry instruction. I was excused due to my wounded hand. Still, while stationed out there, I received the wound medal, the Silver Panzer Badge, and the Iron Cross 1st class.

Then, one day, all the crews were summoned. The Russians had, suddenly and violently, counterattacked, breaking through our defenses and destroying most of our armored vehicles. Our mission to rescue our comrades in Budapest had been reduced to nothing. As a result, all we could do was retreat, in a series of movements, partly on foot and partly in vehicles, to Austria.

Collection of items from Kurt Arp, notably his *Wehrpass* (paybook) and War Merit Cross (*Kriegsverdienstkreuz*), his original armband and a plaque decorated with the division's death's head insignia.

Aftermath

On May 8, 1945, the bulk of the division arrived at the demarcation line. Driven by despair and the obsessive fear of falling into Soviet hands, the Waffen-SS forced the barricade but were stopped a few kilometers farther on by U.S. tanks blocking the way. The troops were disarmed and rounded up in a valley. Up to 90 percent of the Totenkopf had managed to cross the demarcation line.

On the May 14, Waffen-SS and Heer troops were marched off in groups of 500, surrounded by tanks of the U.S. 11th Armored Division. From the start, American officers let them know that anyone trying to escape would be shot. The march quickly turned into a nightmare. Exhausted by the pace set by tanks, and weak from lack of food, many soldiers fell by the side of the road and were shot on the spot by American guards. Arriving at Pregarten, the German troops were met by a Soviet political commissar roaring in a loudspeaker, "None of you will ever go back!" Most of the captives were transported by boat to Odessa and from there to Siberia. Some were released in 1955. Others, less fortunate, never came back.

The graves of three members of the 3rd SS Panzer Regiment Totenkopf.

The final word belongs to Walter Weber:

> I was luckier than my comrades. As we had no real wheeled vehicles—cars, trucks, etc.—our journey to Austria was slow, but we finally made it to Ritzing, near Oberpullendorf. There, finally, the Russians were stopped again, but the front between East and West had been considerably reduced. And, again, we had our infantry training. We would be engaged in fighting in Zöbing am Kamp, and then Säusenstein, on the Danube. We were still waiting for new panzers, but didn't believe we would ever get them. So, it was a surprise when, on May 3, 1945, we were one of ten crews called to pick up brand-new tanks straight from the factory at Saint Valentin. We drove there in trucks that evening, and picked up the tanks the next morning, returning quickly, as the Americans were fast approaching. Everything we had and needed could be taken on board our new Panzer IVs—they felt like luxury palaces to us!
>
> On May 5, we heard gunfire in the west. It grew steadily louder, even as we were driving east to our new positions at the front. When we arrived, we didn't know what was going on, but it seemed to us like everything was coming to an end.
>
> On May 7, we were stationed in a village where everyone was on edge. You could have cut the atmosphere with a knife. Then, we received an order to allow the Americans to pass without resisting! We were stunned, but thankfully no Americans appeared, just a few planes overhead.
>
> On the evening of May 8, we were informed that the German Army had capitulated. The war was over. And yet, for our part, we did not feel like we had been defeated. Where we were stationed, the Russians were in charge, so we decided to scuttle our new tanks to keep them out of the Soviet hands, then head for the American zone in three trucks, then finish the journey on foot. We had until midnight to reach the demarcation line.
>
> With one of my comrades, we walked for many days, only experiencing a couple of incidents along the way—notably scuffles with freed Polish prisoners armed with rifles—but without encountering any Americans. I made it to Mülhausen in Thuringia, and my friend, to Cologne. We had nothing in terms of civilian life—we would have to build new lives with only courage and the strength of our youth.

A group photo of the veterans of the 3rd SS Panzer Regiment Totenkopf. At the very top, from right to left: Kurt Söhrmann and his sister, Pierre Tiquet and Alfred Genath. On the far right in a blue cap is Norbert Hartmann, the last president of the SS Panzer Regiment 3 Veterans' Association. In front, next to Hans Findeisen (in check shirt), is Adolf Suwe's widow. All contributed to the writing of this book by providing photos, stories and documents.

A 3rd SS Panzer Regiment veterans' reunion. Norbert Hartmann, president of the association, stands next to author Pierre Tiquet. Sitting, from right to left, are Kurt Söhrmann, Ernst Walter Kirsch, and Kurt Arp.

Sources

Over the years I got to know the surviving veterans of the 3rd SS Panzer Regiment Totenkopf at their annual reunions. They confided in me their memoirs and photographs and entrusted me to share their experiences with the wider world. For the most part, these men were just 18 years old when they were engaged in World War II, their youth lost to the horror of combat.

Further Reading

Fey, Will, *Armor Battles of the Waffen-SS 1943–45* (translated by H. Henschler), J. J. Fedorowicz Publishing, Manitoba, Winnipeg 1990

Glantz, David M., *When Titans Clashed: How the Red Army Stopped Hitler*, University Press of Kansas, Lawrence, Kansas, 2015

Guderian, Heinz, *Panzer Leader*, E.P. Dutton & Co., New York 1952

Healy, Mark, *Zitadelle: The German Offensive Against the Kursk Salient 4–17 July 1943*, The History Press, Stroud, 2016

Jentz, Thomas, *Panzer Truppen: 1943–1945*, Schiffer Publishing Ltd. (U.S.), Atglen 1998

Lawrence, Christopher, *The Battle of Prokhorovka: The Tank Battle at Kursk, the Largest Clash of Armor in History*, Stackpole Books, Mechanicsburg, Pennsylvania, 2019

Mellenthin, F. W. von, *Panzer Battles: A Study of Employment of Armor in the Second World War*, University of Oklahoma Press, Oklahoma 1956

Raus, Peter Erhard, *Panzer on the Eastern Front 1941–1945*, Greenhill, London 2002

Toeppel, Roman, *Kursk 1943: The Greatest Battle of the Second World War*, Helion and Co., Solihull, 2018

Tucker-Jones, Anthony, *Images of War: Armoured Warfare and the Waffen-SS 1944–1945*, Pen and Sword, Barnsley 2017

Williamson, Gordon, *The Waffen-SS*, Vols 1 & 2, Osprey, Oxford 2003/4

Index